Tamm's Textb

MW01172330

AP* United States History student workbook
for use with Kennedy & Cohen's
The American Pageant†

17th edition

Coursepak Series A   Independently made

David Tamm

*Advanced Placement program and AP are registered trademarks of the College Board, which was not involved in the production of, and does not endorse, this product.

†The American Pageant 17th edition is written by David M. Kennedy, Lizabeth Cohen and Thomas A. Bailey, and published by Cengage. These parties were not involved in the production of, and do not endorse, this product.

Copyright © 2021

CONTENTS

This resource book is organized in the following
way to integrate with Kennedy, Cohen and Bailey's 17th edition:

Suggested Year and Weekly Plan

Vocab and Chapter Assignments

Addenda: Crash Course, Test Correction Forms, Movie Review Forms & More

LICENSING

When given as a full workbook, this material improves content coherency, student enjoyment, parent appreciation, and teacher satisfaction."

-State of Florida Certified Teacher

"Sublimely usable."

"Great as weekly assignments"

"Spend one hour's pay, save 300 hours' planning time!"

"Rocket into the

"Textbooks are expensive. With this workbook, you get your money's worth!"

frontier of utility!"

"They read the book, which is the main issue many have."

"Perfect if there's a substitute"

"Very progressive."

Suggested Year Plan

The ongoing issue with *The American Pageant* is its number of chapters. Most schools begin in late August or early September, leaving ~30 weeks to get through the book if you want any time for review before the exam. Yet there are 40 chapters in the 17th edition of the *Pageant* book, down from 47 in the original 1956 edition and 41 in the 16th edition, but still not whittled down enough to fit a standard-length course, especially if you want to enjoy the semblance of military-style structure. This means it is up to the individual teacher to combine 10 or so chapters. Some give out that amount as a summer assignment. But if you can't or don't do that, know that the period before Jamestown and the period after 1980 don't constitute a great part of the test each. What follows is the 17th edition's contents, and at right, a blast from the past- how this course was ordered when it was young:

The American Pageant 17th edition
Bailey/Kennedy/Cohen, 2020
Weekly Breakdown

A History of Our Country
David S. Muzzey, 1942
Flashback

Week	The American Pageant 17th edition	A History of Our Country
Week 1: Ch. 1	New World Beginnings	Europe Wakes and Stretches
Week 2: Ch. 2	The Contest for North America	A Century of Exploration
Week 3: Ch. 3	Settling the English Colonies	The English Settlements
Week 4: Ch. 4	American Life in the 17th Century	Colonial America
Week 5: Ch. 5	Colonial Society on the Eve	Liberty or Loyalty?
Week 6: Ch. 6	The Road to Revolution	Washington Sees it Through
Week 7: Ch. 7	America Secedes from the Empire	Confederation and Constitution
Week 8: Ch. 8	Confederation and Constitution	Launching the Government
Week 9: Ch. 9	Launching the New Ship of State	Jefferson makes a Great Bargain
Week 10: Ch. 10	The Jeffersonian Republic	Our Second War for Independence
Week 11: Ch. 11	War of 1812 and Nationalism	Sectional Rivalry
Week 12: Ch. 12	Rise of Mass Democracy	The Jacksonian Era
Week 13: Ch. 13	Forging the National Economy	Advance to the Pacific
Week 14: Ch. 14	Ferment of Reform and Culture	The Businessman's Peace
Week 15: Ch. 15	The South and Slavery	The House Divided
Week 16: Ch. 16	Manifest Destiny and Its Legacy	The Civil War
Week 17: Ch. 17	Renewing the Sectional Struggle	Reconstruction
Week 18: Ch. 18	Drifting Towards Disunion	The New Industrial Age
Week 19: Ch. 19	Girding for War: North and South	Futile Party Battles
Week 20: Ch. 20	The Furnace of Civil War	The Rising of the West
Week 21: Ch. 21	The Ordeal of Reconstruction	Dominion Over Palm and Pine
Week 22: Ch. 22	The Industrial Era Dawns	The Roosevelt Era
Week 23: Ch. 23	Political Paralysis in the Gilded Age	The Progressive Movement
Week 24: Ch. 24	America Moves to the City	Wilson and the 'New Freedom'
Week 25: Ch. 25	Conquest of the West	The Struggle for Neutrality
Week 26: Ch. 26	Rumbles of Discontent	Our Part in the Fighting
Week 27: Ch. 27	Empire and Expansion	Influence of the War on Life
Week 28: Ch. 28	Progressivism and Roosevelt	Our Part in the Peace
Week 29: Ch. 29	Wilsonian Progressivism	The Aftermath of the War
Week 30: Ch. 30	American Life in the Roaring '20s	The Program of 'Normalcy'
Week 31: Ch. 31	Great Depression and New Deal	Worshipping the Golden Calf
Week 32: Ch. 32	FDR and the Shadow of War	The Eclipse of Prosperity
Week 33: Ch. 33	American in WWII	The 'Hundred Days'
Week 34: Ch. 34	The Cold War Begins	The New Deal on Trial
Week 35: Ch. 35	American Zenith	Entering a New Decade
Week 36: Ch. 36	The Stormy Sixties	
Week 37: Ch. 37	A Sea of Troubles	
Week 38: Ch. 38	The Resurgence of Conservatism	
Week 39: Ch. 39	Confronting the Post-Cold War Era	
Week 40: Ch. 40	Americans Face a New Century	

Suggested Weekly Plan

Manic Moon Day

It is recommended that students have a lecture overview of the key points in each chapter, take notes, and discuss the concepts involved. Even though teachers are discouraged in parts of the country from lecturing, the speed of the AP* U.S. History course necessitates some direct teacher-student transmission of content. The chapter assignment forms presented herein could be used as a guide during the discussion.

Textbook Tiw's Day

Most school districts encourage pair or group work. This can be used to positive effect if students mine the textbook (or a review book) in class and either jigsaw the chapter, presenting their take on part of the whole, or jointly venture to find the answers to the specific problems in history. The activities herein lend themselves to this kind of classroom setting too. Groups can, for example, take part of each chapter assignment and focus on that, and then discuss their part whole group.

Writing Woden's Day

The AP* U.S. History curriculum is reading and writing intensive, and brainstorming (diagramming) solutions to mini-FRQs is a good way to build up key thinking processes helpful in expressing oneself in writing. Another helpful way is practicing good old-fashioned reading comprehension, but as many teachers know, the content of the passages is key to student growth and success. The material has to be interesting, and luckily, U.S. History has a great potential interest value. If you find the current materials helpful and of high enough quality, you may want to obtain the companion volume to this book, *Tamm's Textbook Tools Coursepak Series B: Reading Shorts, Writings and Online Activities*, on *Amazon.com* or another platform.

Technetronic Thor's Day

Many AP* teachers try to bring in technology to the classroom, whether in the form of a laptop cart, or by taking students to a media lab. Increasingly, students are using their own mobile devices. A good directory to websites usable with AP U.S. History classes, including the Bailey textbook site with history activities, is located at Antarcticaedu.com/US.htm. Included in the addendum to this volume is a Crash Course viewer response sheet that can be given as homework on Thursday nights, or completed as an in-class review assignment.

Fantastic Frija's Day

It is suggested that students take a 25-50-question test once a week. That means a couple chapters might have to be doubled up. A timed, 35 min. period should be reserved in class- or in some cases out depending on how nice you are- to do a weekly 50 question test. If this happens on Friday, it is recommended students take home the chapter assignments for the next week's chapter, or at least part of it, for homework. Doing just the vocab, for example, is itself is a good way to introduce a new chapter.

Important note: Be sure to emphasize to students using this workbook that looking up answers online as to the significance of the vocab terms is not only a cheat, but doesn't work because the AP curriculum assigns a very specific significance to each term, in the context of the course. American Pageant emphasizes that particular significance, in order.

Now let's get down to business!

Quote 4: To the king and queen of which country is Columbus speaking? _____ (pg. 14)

Graph 5: Choose the longer period in time:

   a. From Columbus to the founding of Virginia   *b. From Virginia to Independence*

If the Colonial era was 169 years long, how long has it been *since* independence? _____

The oldest mountains in the Americas are: _____

Canadian Shield _____

'Tidewater' _____

'Roof of America' _____

Did glaciers cover *your* state during the Ice Age?   *a. Yes   b. No   c. I don't live in the USA*

Describe the process by which the Great Lakes formed: The Great Lakes are easily recalled by the mnemonic device HOMES:

_____

_____   **H**   **M**

_____   **O**   **E**

                                                   S

_____ is the 'leftover' lake that is the remnant of Lake Bonneville.

Bering Strait _____

The migrant ancestors of the Indians: *a. arrived all at one time   b. arrived over centuries*

Map 6: During the Ice Age there was   *a. more   b. less*   land than there is today.

Recalling the water cycle from science class, why do you think this is so? Where *was* the missing water?

_____

Incas _____

Mayans _____

Aztecs (Mexica) _____

Maize _____

Map 7: Monster's – oops, that's *Munster's* map – dates from the year _____.

Name three islands marked in the Caribbean Sea:

| North America is distorted and its size is

    a. too small   *b. too large*

Pic 8: This 'corn god' is from the Moche culture of Peru. Which major culture lived in Peru after the Moche?

| Describe how the Aztecs honored their gods:

Pueblo _____

Nation-State _____

Mound-Builders _____

Cahokia _____

Anasazi _____

Three-sister farming _____

Hiawatha _____

Describe the basic lifestyle of the native peoples of North America:

Map 9: Relate the names of the tribes in each region:

Arctic & Subarctic	*Northwest Coast*	*California*	*Plateau*

Great Plains	*Great Basin*	*Northeast*	*Southwest*

Which tribes are nearest to the part of the country you live? | The overall population in 1492 is estimated
| to have been:
|
|_____
|
| Is that more or less than in your *state*?
|
|

Pic 10: Sketch out the
broad outlines of
Cahokia at right, and
Be sure to include
the central building,
lakes, etc.:

The large U.S. city closest to
Cahokia's earthen mound, is: _____

Why do historians believe Leif Eriksson and the Scandinavian Vikings arrived on the shores of
'Vinland' 500 years before Columbus- and the reasons they didn't they stay?

Map 11: What does the orange area   Which European explorer made it to India to establish
on the map signify?   a trade route for spices?

_____   _____

List the major spices Europeans were looking for: _____

Middlemen

Caravel

Pic 12: Marco Polo is shown here in a caravel,   Pic 13: Why did they call this the 'Door of No
What animals did he bring with him?   Return?'

_____   _____

Why did the Arab slave traders sell   Why did slave brokers mix people from different
captives caught far away for higher prices?   regions?

Plantation

'Dark Continent'

Ferdinand of Aragon

Isabella of Castile

Islamic forces from North Africa conquered much of Spain in 711. Christians called the eventual driving out of the Muslims the 'Reconquista,' accomplished by Ferdinand and Isabella in 1492. Why did they 'buy in' to Columbus outlandish idea of sailing directly out into the ocean sea?

Columbian Exchange

Columbus was from this place: *He thought he was going to:*   *He arrived in the Americas on:*

The diffusion of crops and animals from one side of the world to the other is called the **Columbian Exchange**. List some of the things brought from each side of the world to the other:

From New World to Old →   ← *From Old World to New*

'Sugar revolution'

Pic 15: The disease that killed many more Aztecs than guns and swords was _____

Contending Voices 16 - Summarize the views of the following:

Juan Gines de Sepulveda   *Bartolome de Las Casas*

With whom do you agree more?

Treaty of Tordesillas

Encomienda

Map 17: Note the major geographical places reached by the following explorers/conquistadors:

Columbus:

Cabot:

Balboa:

Vespucci:

De Leon:

Cabeza de Vaca:

Pizzaro:

Coronado:

De Soto:

Hernań Corteś

Malinche (Dona Marina)

Tenochtitlan

Conquistador

Moctezuma

Quetzalcoatl

Noche triste

Mexico City

Pg. 18: What are some of the things the Spanish Conquistadors did to become 'Makers of America?'

Capitalism

Mestizos

Dia de la Raza

Pic 20: This large city called _____, was built by the _____.

This space intentionally left empty. Feel free to doodle →

Polytheism is the belief in many gods, monotheism is the belief in one God, and atheism is the belief in the nonexistence of god(s). Which of these three best characterizes the Mesoamericans?

Summarize the *tools* used by the Spaniards to defeat the Aztecs:

Battle of Acoma _____

Pope's Rebellion _____

Kiva _____

Robert de la Salle _____

Black Legend _____

Map 22: While Ponce de Leon searched for the Fountain of Youth and found Florida (to which many elderly people go today to seek a healthy and youth-inspiring climate), what was Coronado searching for, and what did he find instead?

Map 22: The Battle of Ancona took place the modern state of _____

Mission San Antonio is on the _____ side of the   What year was El Paso founded?
Rio Grande River, meaning it is in modern day Texas.

_____

Mission _____

Junipero Serra _____

Map 23: Of the horses that came from Spain,	Note the diffusion paths of the horses that came
Note below the step-by-step diffusion according	from England, France and the Netherlands,
To geographic location:	in terms of which city / port in America they
	were deposited at:
	From France:
	From England:
	From Netherlands:

If we name our first colony on Mars after Captain Kirk, will it be called Jamestown too?

Quote 26: What was Walter Raleigh determined to do?

_____

Huguenots _____

Edict of Nantes _____

Note the significance of the journeys of:

Jacques Cartier: *Samuel de Champlain:*

Coureurs de bois _____

Buccaneers _____

Map 27: The European power that did not yet have a foothold somewhere in North America was:

| Pic 27: Sketch the Iroquois town to
| present to your commanding officer:
|
a. France   *b. Russia* |
|
c. Spain   *d. England* |

Voyageurs _____

Pic 28: The themes in this image are:

a. Social and economic

b. Cultural and geographical

c. All of the above

| Map 29: The modern U.S. states with the most
| French-named cities are most likely:
|
| *a. New York and Virginia*
|
| *b. Michigan and Wisconsin*
|

Pic 30: One reason this is called the "Armada Portrait" is because of its effective use of propaganda portraying the queen as a serene, sovereign power in her own right. Speaking of right, what does she have underneath her right hand- and what do you think it means?

_____

Protestant Reformation _____

Roanoke Island _____

The Spanish Armada _____

Pg. 31 Contending Voices:

Hakluyt's View: **Percy's View:**

What do you think accounts most for the <u>difference</u> in the views of Hakluyt and Percy?

_____

William Shakespeare called England the _____

How did _enclosure_ affect the country socially?

Primogeniture _____

Joint-Stock Company _____

Pic 32: Sir Walter Raleigh wrote one of the first world history books of modern times while he was in prison in the Tower of London. Why was the queen so mad at him?

_____

Virginia Company _____

Charter _____

Jamestown _____

Describe some of the challenges the Jamestown colonists faced when they arrived in 1607:	Why does the book say the 'buzzards' made out well?

Captain John Smith _____

The first 'law' made by the English in North America was: "He who shall not _____, shall not _____." What is your opinion on this law from the perspective of today?

_____

Map 33: At right, sketch the craggy coast of Chesapeake Bay and place the English settlements of the 17th century:

Pic 34: Relate the story of Pocahontas, her background, significance in history, and what became of her:

_____

_____

_____

_____

_____

Powhatan _____

Lord De La Warr _____

1st Anglo-Powhatan War _____

2nd Anglo-Powhatan War _____

Summarize some reasons the Dutch Republic of the Netherlands experienced a 'little golden age' in the 17th century:

_____

Henry Hudson _____

Dutch West India Company _____

Map 36: At right, make a rough sketch of the various colonies, label the rivers and geographical features, note the names of the Indian tribes in the area, and
dot the towns:

Most modern observers would call the deal whereby the Dutch bought Manhattan Island from the local Indians:

    a. fair and square   *b. a total rip-off*

Before it was called New York City, it was called:

_____

Patroonships _____

Pic 36: The woman pictured probably obtained her dress, jewelry, fan and rug from

a. trade with the Bay Colony   *b. trade with local Indians*   *c. Dutch East Indian Company merchants*

Why was the original wall that gave its name to modern Wall Street built?

Pic 37: If you were down and out looking for a job, and saw an ad in a window offering voyages and jobs in a faraway land, to which of the following would you consider going?	Western Australia:	*Definitely*	*Maybe*	*No*
	New Netherland:	*Definitely*	*Maybe*	*No*
	Colony on the Moon:	*Definitely*	*Maybe*	*No*

Quote 38: What kinds of resources did the Narragansetts have access to?

Where did Lake Huron, one of the five Great Lakes, get its name?

Describe why the Swedish colony in Delaware ended:	Instant karma: describe why the Dutch colony ended:

Pg. 40: Make a list of some of the things the Iroquois did to become 'Makers of America?'

Better grab your Penn and get started Pilgrim, or you'll be Quakin', 'cause the Acts of Toleration don't cover sloth! Seriously. They don't.

John Rolfe

Tobacco

Some nicknames for tobacco were: | The first transport of Africans to Virginia was
                                                | in the year:
                                                |

House of Burgesses

What was King James' opinion of the House of Burgesses?   How did he act on this opinion?
                                                            |
                                                            |
                                                            |

Lord Baltimore

Maryland was established as a safe(er) place for: *Puritans   Anglicans   Catholics*

The workers brought over to work on Maryland's | What did it mean to be 'indentured?'
tobacco farms were primarily: |
                                                   |
                                                   |
                                                   |

Act of Toleration

Some Americans today argue that America 'is a Christian country.' If you were a lawyer, how might
you use the circumstances surrounding the Act of Toleration as evidence of the following:

America is (or was) a country for Christian   *America is not (or was not) a country or Christians*
                                            |
                                            |
                                            |
                                            |

Pic 46: Why was sugarcane considered a 'rich man's   How does this picture support that idea?
crop' as opposed to tobacco, the 'poor man's crop? |
                                                       |
                                                       |
                                                       |
                                                       |

Quote 46: Describe the punishment schedule for African slaves on Barbados in the 17th century:

Barbados Slave Code _____

English Civil War _____

The Stuart king _____ was (rather shockingly) executed by _____.

After a decade or so, the Stuart dynasty was restored when _____ was made king.
How did the restoration of the Stuarts influence the colonizing of the Carolinas?

_____

Charles Town (Charleston) _____

Squatters _____

Map 48: This river formed the border between the Carolina and Georgia colonies _____

Tuscarora War _____

What does it mean to say that Georgia was a 'buffer' colony? (It did not mean it worked out more):

_____

James Oglethorpe _____

Calvinism _____

Institutes of the Christian Religion _____

Predestination _____

Conversion _____

'Visible saints' _____

Puritans _____

Separatists _____

Pilgrims _____

Mayflower _____

Pic 51: In this image, I would rather be:

a. The people walking to the ship to go to the New World   _b. The guy in the background_

Myles Standish _____

_____

Plymouth Rock

Mayflower Compact

Quote 51: What is the meaning of William Bradford's words in 'plain Englishe'?

Thanksgiving Day

The Plymouth Colony can best be described as: *a. a Christian colony*   *b. economically attractive*

Massachusetts Bay Company

Great English Migration

John Winthrop

What do you think Winthrop meant by the statement that America "shall be as a city upon a hill?"

What did male property holders able to do that the rest of the Bay Colony was not?

Map 52 (left): List the names of the shires of England from which most of the Puritans set out:

Chances are if you look at a map of Massachusetts, you will find all these names there too:

a. True   b. False   c. Never saw an atlas

Map 52 (right): The destinations in the Americas of the most British migrants, in order of volume, are:

Protestant Ethic

How did the poem *Day of Doom* describe the fate of the damned?

| How might the rules at your school change if it came under Puritan administration?

Quakers

Antinomianism

Pic 54: List some ways in which Anne Hutchinson was a tough and defiant lady: | What terrible fate
 | awaited her in the end?
 |
 |
 |
 |
 |

Roger Williams

Rhode Island's capital is called 'Providence.' What was the meaning of this to the settlers? | Note reasons other settles found the
 | Connecticut River valley attractive:
 |
 |
 |

Fundamental Orders

Map 55: Sketch out and label the colored blobs representing the New England colonies, note the years of establishment, include the rivers that run through them, and dot the towns:

Wampanoag

Massasoit

Pequot War

Pic 56: Why did the Puritan militia and their Narragansett allies attack the Pequot Fort as shown?

Metacom (King Philip)

King Philip's War

How many English settlements were burned down during King Philip's War? | What was Metacom's fate?
 |
 |
 |

New England Confederation

Why were Bay Colony authorities upset with King Charles II in the 1680s?	Why was the Dominion of New England concept also disliked by the Bay Colony's leaders?

Table 57: Note the sovereigns of the Stuart dynasty in England and their relation to America:

1)

2)

l)

3)

4)

5)

Navigation Laws

Sir Edmund Andros

Glorious Revolution

Document 58: Find in the document five words that if you wrote them the way they are there in your English class, your teacher would mark wrong and how you would correct it:

Old fashioned spelling/grammar	*How you would correct it*

1)

2)

3)

4)

5)

'Salutary neglect'

Quakers

Why'd Quakers 'quake'? (You always wanted to know; you just didn't know you wanted to know):

Society of Friends

Pic 59: Adjectives that describe the Quaker lifestyle. Ready go:

| The chances that you will be a Quaker
| for Halloween next year are:
|
| *1 2 3 4 5 6 7 8 9 10*
|

William Penn

Pic 60: Did 'Penn's Woodland' with its City of Brotherly Love (also known as _____)
live up to its promise of openness to differences in settlers and good relations with the Indians? If
you were a lawyer arguing yes and then no, what would be your 'exhibits' and evidence?

Yes it did   *No it didn't*

Bonus points: You may remember from World History class (ah... the memories... loved that
class!) that the ancient river valleys attracted the first settled civilizations, such as the Sumerians,
Egyptians, Harappan Indians and Ancient Chinese. How did rivers play a similar role in America?

What do you think the textbook authors mean when they say the Middle Colonies represent'd a
'Middle Way?'

Pg. 62: Examining the Evidence. What about American history does this item illuminate?

Pg. 63: Varying Viewpoints. If you were a lawyer convincing a jury of the following, what evidence would you bring up to support your argument?

America is a branch of European culture   **America is its own unique culture**

Let's see what it was like!

Today we will be pioneers ourselves, to the most historic places in early America: Jamestown, Plymouth Colony, Boston, and St. Augustine.

Google search: *Jamestown, VA.* Click 'maps' and then click the box that says 'satellite image.' Zoom in a few clicks towards 'Historic Jamestowne' until you are close up to the area between the two rivers. Draw a tourist map of the area below, for someone who will be walking around on foot without GPS. Be sure to label the James River (the big one on the left) and the Back River. Label the streets, such as Colonial Pkwy, and the important buildings:

Google search: *Plymouth Rock, MA.* Click 'maps' and then click the box that says 'satellite image.' Zoom in (or out) a few clicks so you can see the downtown. Draw a tourist map of the area below, for someone who will be walking around on foot without GPS. Be sure to label Plymouth Rock and the Statue of the Forefathers, as well as the streets, such as Main, and the important buildings:

Take the little yellow guy and drag him to Plymouth rock. Walk around a bit until you find the actual rock. What does it say on it?

Google search: *Boston, MA.* Click 'maps' and then click the box that says 'satellite image.' Zoom in (or out) a few clicks so you can see the downtown centered around Boston Common. Draw a tourist map of the area below, for someone who will be walking around on foot without GPS. Be sure to label Boston Common, Old North Church, the Paul Revere House and the other sites, as well as the streets, such as Main, and the important buildings:

Now, click the little yellow person and drag him to Salem St. by Old North Church to get a street view. Walk around a bit.

What is going on around you? | What color are the buildings?

Google search: *St. Augustine, FL.* Click 'maps' and then click the box that says 'satellite image.' Zoom in (or out) a few clicks so you can see the downtown centered around Ponce DeLeon's Fountain of Youth. Draw a tourist map of the area below, for someone who will be walking around on foot without GPS. Be sure to label the Fountain of Youth, the Castillo de San Marcos, the Lightner Museum, as well as the streets, and the important buildings:

Finally, search: **Rocket Garden Kennedy Space Center.** Drag your yellow guy to the Rocket Garden and look around. What do you see around you?

YOU BE THE JUDGE **Name** _____

"Wow, this is like an academic great awakening."

Attorney	*Defender*	*Defense*	*Jury*	*Magistrate*	*Plaintiff*	*Prosecutor*	*Verdict*

Trial terms: _____ 1. Another word for judge. _____ 2. Synonym for lawyer.

_____ 3. The lawyer who defends. _____ 4. Lawyer trying to convict.

_____ 5. People who judge a case. _____ 6. The decision of the court.

_____ 7. Side bringing the charge. _____ 8. Side that is on trial.

Trial: **John Winthrop and the Ministers of the Church of Boston *v.* Anne Hutchinson (1637)**

Charges: **1) Defaming the ministers of Boston and their ministry; 2) Heresy**

Reporter: Good evening, I am standing here in front of the courthouse in Boston, where Anne Hutchinson is on trial for damaging the reputation of the ministers of the Puritan church. The Massachusetts Bay Colony was founded here 17 years ago by the Pilgrims, when they landed at Plymouth Rock after having fled England on the Mayflower to escape religious persecution. While the Colony was founded so that the Puritans could practice their own faith, now it seems religious liberty for people who believe differently may not be part of the plan. Let's listen in on the court.

Baliff: Here ye here ye, aw yay aw yay, please rise for the honorable, the judge John Winthrop.

Judge Winthrop: Defendant, raise your right hand. Do you swear to tell the truth, the whole truth, and nothing but the truth, so help you God?

Anne Hutchinson: I do.

Reporter: Ladies and gentlemen, according to our sources, Anne is an herbal healer and common housewife who arrived in this colony three years ago. In that time, she held popular religious meetings in her home, where 80 or so people would gather for Bible readings and to study sermons given by the colonial ministers the previous day. Unlike in other places and in other times, people here don't go to church just on Sunday- they go every day. Usually, in a court of law, the judge and the prosecuting attorney are not the same person, but in this case, they are.

Prosecutor: Mrs. Hutchinson, you are called here as someone who has disturbed the peace of the colony by speaking of diverse things prejudicial to the honor of the Puritan church and her goodly ministers. You have held meetings and classes that have been condemned as intolerable to the sight of God, and not befitting for a woman to hold. After all, while all those people attend your meetings, they most certainly are not working diligently or keeping their houses.

Anne Hutchinson: Yes, I have been called before this court, but I hear no actual charges against me. What have I done? Since times of yore, elder women have often been called on to instruct younger women- and men- as I have.

Prosecutor: Oh, the examples are many! Our pure doctrine emphasizes the performance of Goodly Works, which are then interpreted as evidence as to whether an individual has been elected for salvation. But isn't it true, Mrs. Hutchinson, that you have been stressing the idea that a person's own spiritual consciousness of God's election might also be evidence for a person's salvation into heaven when they break the surly bonds of this Earthly life?

Anne Hutchinson: It is true. I believe- like the minister John Cotton- that the Puritan doctrine of 'Goodly Works' doesn't alone justify salvation of the Elect, because all people may have the Holy Ghost dwelling inside of them, and if they are but conscious of it, that spirit can also help them understand themselves to be among the Elect of God.

Prosecutor: I call Minister John Cotton to the stand. Minister Cotton, what do you have to say about Anne Hutchinson?

John Cotton: She is a deeply spiritual, wonderful woman and mother, who has borne fourteen children, and cares deeply about our colony and its people. She wants to see Massachusetts Bay succeed and grow in this new land. She doesn't slander the ministers in her meetings, she discusses what they have said and the gathered people comment as they see fit. Indeed, her meetings are in private, not in public, and I believe she has a right to hold them. Also, for the record, I do not see any clear witness against her, and you know it is a rule of the court that no man may be a judge and an accuser too. She has not broken any law of God or country, and therefore deserves no censure.

Prosecutor: This court is not interested in whether the meetings took place in public or in private. She is a dissenter, whom seven ministers have declared said that ministers are wrong to preach the 'Doctrine of Good Works' only, and because this is so, therefore they are not able ministers of the gospel! Did she not say these things?

John Cotton: She did. She spoke to the assembled about these matters, but also to the ministers themselves.

Anne Hutchinson: I was reluctant to speak with the ministers about these private topics, but they wanted me to, and I did, in confidence. That confidence was broken by them when they brought these charges against me. I ask the court to have them testify under oath that they promised me our conversations were to be kept in the strictest confidence.

Judge: This court has heard enough. Mrs. Hutchinson, you say this 'Free Grace' doctrine of yours can potentially make you one of the Elect, fully apart from our traditional belief in 'Good Works' as sole evidence of heavenly virtue. This doctrine in itself is damaging enough to our community. Indeed, Anne, you the cause of all our troubles. You are a heretic and an instrument of the Devil. And as such, it pleased the Lord to hear the prayers of us, his afflicted people. And through the care and endeavor of the wise and faithful ministers of the Boston Church, assisted by the civil authority of Boston town, we have hereby discovered you to be a masterpiece of the Old Serpent. We have done the Lord's work, and it is marvelous before our eyes. Now we must consider what is to be done with you. Anne Hutchinson, this court finds you guilty of slander and heresy. It is our verdict that you withdraw yourself out of our Congregation, and like a leper, leave the colony for good. This court is adjourned.

Reporter: Quite a spectacle here in Boston, where Anne has just been both excommunicated from the Puritan congregaton and ordered into exile from Massachusetts Bay. Will her husband and children go with her? Wait! There is some commotion going on as the bailiff escorts Anne out of the court. A woman, Mary Dyer, is running up to her. She's taken Anne's hand in solidarity. The two women are approaching the large metal doors. Wait a minute, Anne is turning around, it looks like she is about to say something. Everybody is silent, you can hear a mouse scurrying.

Anne Hutchinson: You have no power over me! You can do no harm to me, for I am in the hands of the Eternal Jehovah. No further do I esteem any mortal man than as a creature in his hand, therefore take heed how you proceed against me, for I know that for what you do to me, God will ruin you, your posterity, and this whole country.

Reporter: Whoa, Anne has just said some seditious things, and brought back the old blood guilt threat to Winthrop's children, and it looks like he's going to find her in contempt of court. This brings up a philosophical question: If someone has been deprived of their citizenship, can they still commit sedition? We'll have to consider that another time. For now, all in all, this has been a trial about freedom of speech and freedom of religion. And it won't be the last. Later this year, my sources tell me, Katherine Finch will be excommunicated by the same court, for the same offense. Two years from now, Phillip Hammond will be excommunicated just for saying, "Anne didn't deserve censure and exile." Nine years in the future, Sarah Keayne will also be exiled for holding religious meetings and "irregularly prophesying." Soon after, Joan Hogg will also be exiled not only for "disorderly singing," but for saying she "heard the voice of Christ telling her what to do." As for Anne herself, she will be killed by Indians in 1643, in what will later become New York state. Let's listen in on the reaction in Boston to the tragic news of her death:

Judge: Let her damned heresies, and the just vengeance of God, by which she perished, terrify all her seduced followers from having any more to do with her ideas.

Reporter: America may be a land of religious freedom and toleration in the far future, but not today. Coming to you from Boston, this is _____ for History Action News. Stay tuned for weather, we'll be right back.

9. The reporter said this trial was about freedom of speech. What does that mean to you?	10. The reporter also said this trial was about freedom of religion. What does that mean to you?	11. This was not a jury trial, but if it it was, would you have found Anne guilty or not guilty?
		_____
		12. A trial with these charges would not take place in modern America. Which Amendment guarantees that?

COLONIAL ART & MUSIC Dynamo_____

What did Colonial Americans listen to? Whatever it was, you better believe it was off the chain

Renaissance Era Music (1600s)	I've heard this!		I like it (1-10)
Virginia Company			
Tobacco	Yes	No	
	_____		_____
Henry Purcell			
Funeral March	Yes	No	
	_____		_____
William Byrd			
The Battle	Yes	No	
	_____		_____
Claudio Monteverdi			
L'Orfeo	Yes	No	
	_____		_____
Jacques Offenbach			
Gallop Infernal	Yes	No	
	_____		_____

Baroque Era Music (1700s)	I've heard this!	I like it (y/n)
Johann Pachelbel		
Canon in D	_____	_____
Johann Sebastian Bach		
Toccata & Fugue in D-Minor	_____	_____
Brandenburg Concerto	_____	_____
George Friedrich Handel		
Fireworks Music	_____	_____
Zadok the Priest	_____	_____
Messiah	_____	_____
Antonio Vivaldi		
The Four Seasons	_____	_____

"If you don't get your head-right and brush those teeth, you're going to get the kind of indenture that doesn't go away!" –Colonial Mom

Quote 68: Bradford does not expressly list this as something afflicting the Pilgrims:

   a. lack of friends   *b. lack of shelter*   *c. tiredness*   *d. lack of clothing*

Life in the early Chesapeake was: *a. really, really tough*   *b. relaxing*

Indentured servants _____

Head-right system _____

Pic 69: Just about the first product that were specifically advertised to target markets was:

Quote 69: The companyman compares Virginia to the: *a. best*   *b. worst*   parts of England.

William Berkeley _____

Nathanial Bacon _____

Bacon's Rebellion _____

Contending Voices 70 – How did each think about the relationship between rulers and ruled:

       Nathanial Bacon   *William Berkeley*

Who do you agree with more?

Examining the Evidence 71 - What did this deal entail?

_____

_____

Thinking Globally 72 – How many Africans died aboard ship or at sea on the way to the Americas? What were the primary cash crops those who lived worked on upon arriving?

Africa has suffered with slavery as perhaps no other continent. To the vast unknown number of people throughout the centuries who have lived as slaves in Africa, add the total number of Africans kidnapped and taken between 700 and 1600 from the East Coast to the Middle East, primarily by Arab slave traders (~12,000,000), to the number taken the West Coast between 1500 and 1850, primarily by European slave traders (~11,000,000), to get a total number of Africans shipped into slavery as somewhere in the vicinity of:

Pic 72: Where are these Africans headed in chains and yokes?

_____

How many in the picture are driving them there, and with what kinds of weapons?

| Pic 73 (bot): On the slave ship, of the slaves transported on the lower deck, how many were either children or Pygmies stored together?

_____

| Why do you think slaves were placed by height?

Royal African Company _____

Middle Passage _____

Slave Codes _____

Quote 75: What argument did the Mennonites of Germantown, PA make against slavery?

| Pic 75: Rice cultivation thrives most under
|
| _a. wet conditions_   _b. dry conditions_
|

Pic 70: The city pictured is _____, from which exports of rice etc. left for England.

At right, draw a triangle with horizontal lines and label the class structure in places like this in and around the Colonial South, in layers:

Pic 77: New England women had an amazing average of _____ children.

   a. six   _b. eight_   _c. ten_

of whom an average of _____ survived.

| Quote 77: How did John White describe
| New England?
|
|
|
|
|
|_____

What were the divorce laws like in New England?

Quote 79: What does the Massachusetts School Law tell us about how the colonists regarded education?

| The oldest college in America is:
|
|
|
| ...founded in the year _____

Pic 79: Like the colonial school children, copy into this space the lessons learned while learning the ABCs:

A)   B)

C)   D)

E)   F)

G)   *As runs the glass, our life doth pass.*   *The rest are online if you search 'In Adam's Fall we sinned all'*

Congregational Church

Jeremiad

Half-Way Covenant

The Elect

Salem Witch Trials

Pic 80: If you were an elderly woman in 17th century England and you saw this dude roll up, you should probably

   a. Answer the door   *b. Run*

| What did the New Englanders believe should be done
| with the land that they criticized the Indians for not
| doing?
|
|
|

Pic 82: Prudence Punderson's painting packed a plethora of powerful pictures into a poignant progression of a person's puttering through past, present and postmortem.

What did the combination of "Calvinism, soil and climate" in New England help encourage in the people?

| How did New England affect the rest
| of the nation's future philosophy?
|
|
|

Leisler's Rebellion

Why don't Dukes emigrate?

"So, there is this shipment of tea due in from India soon, want to…"

Quote 84: To Sam Adams, what did America allow for that others places in the world didn't?

| Of all Britain's _____ colonies in the
| America's, this many would join to rebel:
|
|

Borderlands

What does the term 'conquest by the cradle' mean and why were the English, like Dr. Johnson, perturbed by it?

| Which (European) races arrived and
| 'mingled' with the English at this point?
|
|
|
|

Map 87: This group especially used the 'great wagon road' to move into the Appalachian backcountry:

| This group moved especially into Pennsylvania:
|
|
| This group remained dominant up the Hudson River
| from New York City:
|

Chart 88: The first U.S. Census taken was in 1790. Replicate the bar graph below

	10%	20%	30%	40%	50%
English					
African					
Scottish					
German					
Scots-Irish					
Irish					
Dutch					
Other Euro					

Proportionally, the English majority had been   *a. rising*   *b. falling*   since the Pilgrims arrived.

Quote 88: What new 'race' did this French writer argue was being created? _____

Paxton Boys

Regulator Movement

As the slave population began including more women from Africa, the proportion of blacks who were born in Africa and transported versus those born in America

a. Grew   *b. Declined*   *c. Stayed the same*

| Some African words in the English
| language today are:
|
|
|
|

New York Slave Revolt

Contending Voices 89 – What were some attitudes about race described by the following:

Samuel Sewall – critic of slavery   *Virginia Slave Code – pro slavery*

Did these entities share any attitudes in common?

South Carolina Slave Revolt

Pg. 90: What are some of the things Africans did to become 'Makers of America'?

If you've read the *Scarlet Letter*, you know Hester Prynne had to wear a large letter *A* for 'adulteress' because she became pregnant while her husband was lost at sea. We've read that a big red letter had to be worn if a person was receiving charity from the taxpaying pubic:

What letter was it? | Today, nearly half of all Americans are on some from of public assistance
(use a nice red crayon or marker if handy) | Would you advocate these people wear a similar badge? Why or why not?

Pic 92: Of which positive features about the new shipment of slaves does this shameful ad boast? | Why did the colonies try to stop slave imports?

| How did the British authorities react?

Out of clerics, physicians and lawyers (jurists), which job was least respected?

_____

Pic 86: The mighty catch was of _____.
The special location off the coast off Cape Cod where the fish were plentiful is called:

_____

Have you ever had cod? Is it good?

| Map 93: Note the economic activities of the following:
|
| *Boston*:
|
| *New York*:
|
| *Philadelphia*:
|
| *Baltimore*
|
| *Norfolk*:
|
| *Charleston*:
|

Triangular trade

Map 94: Complete the items transported by triangle trade for the following empires, inc. arrows:

England | Spain / Portugal

English Colonies | Latin | America

West Africa | West Africa

Molasses Act

Road conditions in America were generally:

a. Surprisingly good   b. Really bad

| While big news can spread from Philadelphia to
| Charleston in less than 1 second today with an
| email or text, Charleston residents didn't know
| about the Declaration of Independence until a
|
| a. Day later   b. Week later   c. Month later
|

Quote 95: Why was Cotton Mather angry at Bostonians?

| Do some people today still reject
| what the Bostonians back then
| were rejecting?

Table 97 (bottom): Note the various denominations and their adherents on the eve of revolution:

Quote 98: What did Ben Franklin mean when he said, "A good example is the best sermon?"	What did he mean when he noted that, "Many quarrel about religion that never practiced it"?

Arminianism

The Great Awakening

Jonathan Edwards

George Whitefield

'Old lights', 'new lights'

Pic 99: Describe a George Whitefield sermon:	Quote 98: In Whitfield's sermon, what does he speak about?
	Some 'new light' colleges that appeared were:

Pic 100: The look of Princeton when it first opened can be best described as: a. Lush and endowed b. Austere and spartan	What was the 'real meaning' that boys learned in these early colleges?

Pic 101: What is the use of this decorated item?

Quote 101: Of the seventeen subjects John Adams mentions he or his sons or grandsons will or may study, order them by how interesting they seem to you:	Adams implies his sons and grandsons will study the things they want because:

Pic 102: Thanks to Ben Franklin's experiments with key and kite, the people shown here are beginning to understand and unlock the secrets of:

_____

_____

Poor Richard's Almanack

In the Almanack shone Franklin's wisdom, but what do you think the statements meant?

SAYING   *MEANING*

*"What maintains one vice would
bring up two children"*   _____

"Plough deep while sluggards sleep"   _____

"Honesty is the best policy"   _____

"Fish and visitors stink in three days"   _____

Zenger Trial

Royal colonies

Proprietary colonies

Why did backcountry people's resentment of | To what extent do you think backcountry
coastal elites increase in the late colonial era? | Americans still resent political elites today?
                                                                              |
                                                                              |
                                                                              |
                                                                              |
                                                                              |

Pic 104: What was the functional purpose of the gear the hunters of early America wore?

_____

Colonial assemblies

Pic 106: Today there are tens of | Note the status in colonial America of the following:
thousands of pool halls all across |
America. Where did this game come from?| *running water:*   *garbage disposal:*
                                                      |
                                                      |
                                                      |

Colonial Vocab Review Name _____

"Wow, this is like an academic great awakening."

Anne Hutchinson	Aristocracy	Boston	Commerce, labor & money	Democratic
Dutch	England	Farming	France	Georgia
Government	Great Awakening	Jamestown	John Winthrop	Massachusetts
Maryland	Mayflower Compact	New York	Pennsylvania	Philadelphia
Pocahontas	Predestination	Quakers	Roanoke	Spain
Squanto	Toleration	Tobacco	Triangle	Virginia

While politics is mostly about _____, economics is mostly about _____.

While _____ claimed the American Southwest, _____ controlled the Mississippi Valley & Canada.

While _____ established the 13 Colonies, the _____ founded New Amsterdam, later New York.

While the 'Lost Colony' of _____ was first, _____ was the first English colony to succeed.

Chief Powhatan's daughter _____ brought food to Jamestown, as _____ did in Plymouth.

John Smith told Jamestown colonists if they do not work they do not eat, while the Pilgrims signed the _____.

While the Pilgrims founded Plymouth as a Puritan religious colony, _____ was founded as a haven for Catholics.

"You can and you can't, you will and you won't, you're damned if you do, and damned if you don't," reflects Puritan _____.

_____ was a famous governor of Massachusetts Bay, who argued America was to be a "City upon a Hill, for all to see."

In Colonial times, modern Vermont was part of _____, Maine was part of _____, and West Virginia was part of _____.

After _____, mother of 14, was exiled from MA for interpreting sermons, her whole family was killed by the Siwanoy Indians.

Rhode Island, founded by the exile Roger Williams, was known for its religious _____ (and for being tiny and cute).

Turning to slave labor, Virginia and other Southern colonies had success in growing John Rolfe's cash crop _____.

The terrible 'Middle Passage,' which saw slaves brought from West Africa to the New World, was the second part of _____ trade.

William Penn was granted a proprietary charter to start this colony, _____, a haven for _____.

Nathanial Bacon led a rebellion against Virginia's upper class _____, while his followers settled _____ North Carolina.

James Oglethorpe obtained a proprietorship for the southernmost colony, _____, named after King George II, not I or III.

During the _____, Whitefield and Edwards helped many Americans go from being very religious to super religious.

Whether free, slave or indentured, man or woman, old or young, even a kid, this was the work most Americans did: _____.

In Colonial times, America's two largest cities, _____, MA and _____, PA, had less than 20,000 people.

From now on you have to pay a quarter for each sheet of paper your teacher gives you. Liking that Stamp Act yet?

Quote 107: Adams says the revolution began before the war started. What do you think he meant by that?

War of Jenkin's Ear _____

King George's War _____

Pic 106: Is this image a perfectly accurate representation of what happened? Why or why not?

_____

Fort Duquesne _____

George Washington _____
(do NOT put something like "First President of the USA"... identify his significance in this chapter!)

Fort Necessity _____

Acadians (Cajuns) _____

French and Indian War _____

Seven Years' War _____

Map 111: During the Seven Year's 'Global' War, the first and last fighting took place on this continent:	How many battles took place in Dutch territory (Netherlands)?

Pic 112: What is the meaning behind Benjamin Franklin's famous *'Don't Tread on Me'* symbol inscribed with *'Join, or Die,'* later adapted for the Gadsden Flag?

_____

Albany Congress _____

Edward Braddock _____

Regulars _____

'Buckskins' _____

William Pitt

James Wolfe

Marquis de Montcalm

Battle of Quebec

Pic 113: Since the British and Scottish Act of Union (1707), the
British identity had formed and the country was called
Great Britain officially. It also flew a new flag, seen here, called
The Union Jack. Draw and shade in the flag if you can, at right:

Note the territorial changes after the French and Indian War regarding the following:

French authority in North America　　　　*France to Spain*　　　　*Spain to Britain*

Map 114: These two rivers became the boundary | Note the location of Russia's holdings:
between British and Spanish America:

Chief Pontiac

Pontiac's War

Proclamation of 1763

Map 117: Sketch the red Proclamation Line of 1763 horozontially across the paper, with north to
the left and south to the right, and a rough draft of the boundaries, rivers and cities east of the
Mississippi:

Republicanism

Radical Whigs

Pic 118: What is "Lady Britain" saying to "Lady America?"

| What does she say in response?

Mercantilism

What did the British do concerning the following that agitated the colonists?

Currency restrictions   Nullification rights   Mercantilist system

Pic 119: Copley's painting of Revere shows a new:

a. Aristocratic spirit   *b. Democratic spirit*   *c. Monarchical spirit*

Sugar Act

George Grenville

Quartering Act

Stamp Act

Admiralty courts

'Guilty until proven innocent'

'No taxation without representation'

Quote 120: What did Edmund Burke tell the young man to expect from America?

| What distinction did Americans make between taxation and legislation?

Stamp Act Congress

Nonimportation agreements

Sons of Liberty

Daughters of Liberty

Pic 121: Sometimes an uproar comes around when people who buy American flags for the Fourth of July or some other holiday look and see their flag was made in China. How is this picture similar when we think about why the Chinese might have made those American flags?

Contending Voices 121 - Summarize the views of the following:

John Dickinson   *Thomas Paine*

Why do you think Paine's advice won out?

Declaratory Act

Townshend Acts

Pic 122: Who is this guy, what is his job, and what the heck are they doing to him?

Pic 123: Do either of these images paint the British in a favorable light? | How do they differ (aside from being 86 years apart)?

Boston Massacre

George III

Lord North

Committees of Correspondence

Pic 124: Some Sam Adams accomplishments: | Some Abigail Adams accomplishments:

Boston Tea Party

Pic 125: As the tea party threw over the tea, and more come to join, what kind of disguises did they wear? | Quote 125: Loyalists like Ann Hulton were getting nervous as revolutionary fervor picked up. What did the Loyalists want to see happen?

Intolerable Acts

Quebec Act

First Continental Congress

The Association

Pic 127: The village green of Concord saw the British drilling. Why were they always called the 'Redcoats?' | What was the 'shot heard round the world' in Emerson's poem?

Lexington and Concord

Minute Men

Quote 128: Edmund Burke has long been a hero to conservatives. What did he want to see happen?

Thinking Globally 130 – How does this article compare the Tupac Amaru situation with the American?

Note the strengths and weaknesses of the imperial British forces and the American forces:

	Strengths	Weaknesses
British		
American		

Marquis de Lafayette _____

Valley Forge _____

Camp followers _____

Lord Dunmore _____

Baron von Steuben _____

Pic 133: There is a famous painting of Washington "Crossing the Delaware" that was in every previous edition of this textbook until this one, the seventeenth. American culture is changing, and textbooks are highlighting previously neglected aspects of U.S. history more and more. Why is this image from the 17th edition a good example of that trend?

Don't write till you see the whites of the blanks where answers should be

1760 – Rigaud surrenders to Amherst sealing a _____ victory in the French & Indian War.

King George II of Great Britain dies, and is succeeded by his son _____

1763 – After the Treaty of Paris makes peace, both the English and French king have lots of war _____

1764 – Parliament passes the _____ Act, which the colonists did not find very sweet at all.

Parliament passes the _____ Act, which prohibited the colonists from minting money.

1765 – Parliament passes the _____ Act, which taxed paper products and led to more unrest.

Parliament passes the _____ Act, which required colonists to house Redcoat soldiers.

1766 - Parliament repeals the Stamp Act, but passes the _____ Act, 'declaring' its supremacy.

This patriotic group raises 'liberty poles' and skirmishes with angry soldiers _____ ____ _____

1767 - Parliament passes the _____ Act, which required colonists to pay import tariffs.

1768 – Colonists _____ British goods after John Hancock's boat in Boston is confiscated.

1770 – The _____ _____ fuels tensions even though John Adams acted as defense.

1773 - Parliament passes the _____ Act, allowing the BEIC to ship tea duty-free to Boston.

Sons of Liberty dressed as Indians threw over 342 chests of tea in the _____

1774 – Parliament passes the Boston Port and Quebec Acts, known to the colonists as _____!

The First _____ _____ organizes an ineffective Petition to the King.

1775 – The midnight ride of _____ _____ warns the colonists of the Redcoat approach.

Battles of _____ __ _____ are the first of the Revolutionary War.

The Battle of _____ _____ gives the colonists confidence in their abilities.

The Second _____ _____ sends the Olive Branch Petition to King George.

1776 – Thomas Paine publishes the pamphlet _____ _____ supporting independence.

Second Continental Congress approves and passes the _____ ____ _____

Boston Massacre	***Boston Tea Party***	***Boycott***	***British***	***Bunker Hill***
Common Sense	***Continental Congress***	***Continental Congress***	***Currency***	***Debt***
Declaratory	***Declaration of Independence***	***George III***	***Intolerable***	***Lexington & Concord***
Quartering ***Paul Revere*** ***Sons of Liberty***		***Stamp***	***Sugar***	***Tea*** ***Townshend***

Ch. 6   **FRENCH & INDIAN WAR: TICKET OUT DA DOOR**   **Victor** _____

Note a Cause: _____

Note a Course (event): _____

Note a Consequence: _____

Ch. 6   **FRENCH & INDIAN WAR: TICKET OUT DEE DOOR**   **Victor** _____

Note a Cause: _____

Note a Course (event): _____

Note a Consequence: _____

Ch. 6   **FRENCH & INDIAN WAR: TICKET OUT DUH DOOR**   **Victor** _____

Note a Cause: _____

Note a Course (event): _____

Note a Consequence: _____

Ch. 6   **FRENCH & INDIAN WAR: TICKET OUT DÉ DOOR**   **Victor** _____

Note a Cause: _____

Note a Course (event): _____

Note a Consequence: _____

Ch. 6   **FRENCH & INDIAN WAR: TICKET OUT DÆ DOOR**   **Victor** _____

Note a Cause: _____

Note a Course (event): _____

Note a Consequence: _____

Ch. 6   **FRENCH & INDIAN WAR: TICKET OUT DË DOOR**   **Victor** _____

Note a Cause: _____

Note a Course (event): _____

Note a Consequence: _____

John Adams ep. 1: Join or Die (12:50 in)

1. When the lawyer John Adams goes to visit Captain Preston and the other Redcoats, what does Preston tell him?

_____

| 2. John Adams' chairs at his house are made of:

   a. Plastic   b. Vinyl   c. Leather

3. During the funeral procession, John tells Sam Adams that he:

   a. Is a Loyalist   b. Is a Patriot

   c. Wants the soldiers to have a fair trial

| 4. During the funeral procession, Sam confronts his cousin John. What organization does he belong to

   The _____ ____ _____

5. During the trial, both sides called eyewitnesses. What did they say?

For the prosecution: *For the defense:*

(Move to 39:40)
6. If you were on the jury, how would you find the defendants? | 7. What was the actual verdict?

a. Guilty of murder   b. Not guilty due to firing in self-defense | _____

Ch. 6   **BOSTON MASSACRE TRIAL**   **Lawyer** _____

John Adams ep. 1: Join or Die (12:50 in)

1. When the lawyer John Adams goes to visit Captain Preston and the other Redcoats, what does Preston tell him?

_____

| 2. John Adams' chairs at his house are made of:

   a. Plastic   b. Vinyl   c. Leather

3. During the funeral procession, John tells Sam Adams that he:

   a. Is a Loyalist   b. Is a Patriot

   c. Wants the soldiers to have a fair trial

| 4. During the funeral procession, Sam confronts his cousin John. What organization does he belong to

   The _____ ____ _____

5. During the trial, both sides called eyewitnesses. What did they say?

For the prosecution: *For the defense:*

(Move to 39:40)
6. If you were on the jury, how would you find the defendants? | 7. What was the actual verdict?

a. Guilty of murder   b. Not guilty due to firing in self-defense | _____

Don't start writing 'till you see the whites of the blanks where answers should be.

Quote 138: What do you think Thomas Paine meant by, "summer soldier and sunshine patriot?"

Second Continental Congress

The Congress wanted a 'redress of grievances' at this point, which best approximated:

a. Giving up   *b. Asking the government to make things right*   *c. Full independence*

Note 10 character traits George Washington had that drove the Congress to give him command?

1   *6*

2   *7*

3   *8*

4   *9*

5   *10*

Pic 139: Who painted this famous painting of Washington? _____

Ethan Allen _____

Benedict Arnold _____

Bunker Hill _____

Olive Branch Petition _____

Hessians _____

Pic 140: What do you think the caption means when it says Americans scored a 'moral victory' even though they had to abandon Bunker and Breed's Hill to the British?

_____

Assault on Quebec _____

Evacuation Day _____

Thomas Paine

Common Sense

Map 141: Note the dates of the following battles and maneuvers:

_____ *Lexington & Concord*	_____ *Long Island*	_____ *Fort Stanwix*
_____ *Battle of Bunker Hill*	_____ *Washington's Retreat*	_____ *Ft. Oriskany*
_____ *Siege of Boston*	12/25/76 ****The Crossing****	_____ *Brandywine*
_____ *Lake Champlain*	_____ *Battle of Trenton*	_____ *Germantown*
_____ *Attack on Quebec*	_____ *Battle of Princeton*	_____ *Monmouth C.H.*

Quote 142 (top): How does Paine feel about monarchy?	Pic 142: Does he *look* like he's *kidding*?
	a. No *b. Actually, kinda*

Quote 142 (bot.): According to Abbe Raynal, are America's principles for rebellious Englishmen alone, or for the oppressed of France as well?	What allusion did Paine make to the force of gravity in his writing?

'Virtue'

Paine's pamphlet got people thinking about a republican form of government, but there was disagreement on whether 'the People' in general, had the civic virtue to make it work. Why do you think civic virtue is necessary in a system like ours?	What did the people who wanted 'natural aristocracy' argue for?

What did delegate Richard Henry Lee, ancestor of Civil War general Robert E. Lee, resolve at the Congress on June 7, 1776, which was adopted on July 2?

Declaration of Independence

Thomas Jefferson

Some of the complaints about the king included:

What similarities are there between Ben Franklin's quote: *"We must all hang together, or we will all hang separately,"* and the statement from the Declaration of Independence: *"We mutually pledge to each other our lives, our fortunes and our sacred honor":*

_____

July 4, 1776

_____

Declaration of the Rights of Man

_____

Pic 144: What has modern science told us about King George III?

_____

Loyalists

_____

Patriots

_____

Pg. 145: Examining the Evidence. What about American history does this item illuminate?

_____

_____

_____

Patrick Henry

_____

How did the colonist rebels reflect the "Anglo-Saxon regard for order" in their treatment of Loyalists?

_____

Battle of Long Island

_____

William Howe

_____

Battle of Trenton

_____

Pic 148: The story of a statue. Note the major events in the bio of this statue:

1766 – Put on a pedestal to honor the king, who:

1776 – Torn down to make _____ *to use on the king's men.*

_____

Pic 149: Well it is here after all isn't it? The Crossing. How was 'The Crossing' of the _____ River instrumental in boosting the Patriot's morale?

Gentleman John Burgoyne

Barry St. Leger

How did Benedict Arnold, whose name is synonymous in America with 'traitor,' due to later defection, get the British to do to win an essential strategic victory with his heroics on the lake?

Saratoga

Horatio Gates

Quote 150: Countries have often used diplomatic recognition as a way to influence and legitimize a new socio-political situation. In 2008, Serbia and Russia were angry when the United States and some others 'recognized' the new state of Kosovo, carved out of Serbia by Albanian migrants who settled there and declared independence. Put another way, if, say, California declared independence from the United States and Mexico and Canada quickly 'recognized' it as a country, it might lead to tension between them and the U.S. How does this quote mirror those situations?

Novus ordo seculorum

Model Treaty

Pic 151: 'America' was not just to be a country, but a new attitude. How did Ben Franklin use dress to demonstrate what that would be to the Europeans?

| What did Franklin do to set a precedent that "practical self-interest" would sometimes trump "abstract idealism?"

Armed Neutrality

Monmouth

Table 152: These countries joined in the war against Britain:

Comte de Rochambeau

How much did the British pay Benedict Arnold to sell out the fort of West Point and go traitor? | At this point, which part of the colonies did the British focus on to 'roll them up' and win?

Battle of King's Mountain

Battle of Cowpens

Nathanial Greene

Charles Cornwallis

Map 153: Lord Cornwallis arrived in Charleston by sea on this date: _____.

He then fought at King's Mountain and Cowpens and arrived in the coastal city: _____.

He then moved north in May 1781 to the emerging state of _____.

These two opponents met Cornwallis at Yorktown _____ & _____.

"Hair buyers"

The "Bloody Year"

Pic 154: Who did Joseph Brant, chief of the _____, side with? _____

Treaty of Ft. Stanwix

George Rogers Clark

Map 154: label the places significant during the George Rogers Clark campaign & the Ohio River:

*

*

*

*

Privateers

Quote 154: How were American soldiers 'different,' according to Baron von Stuben? | Pic 155: Describe the importance of the Battle of the Chesapeake Capes:

Admiral de Grasse

Battle of Yorktown

'The World Turn'd Upside Down'

'No Quarter for the Tories!'

Contending Voices 156 – What did the following say about how the American Revolution was different than the French Revolution, which began 8 years after Yorktown?

Friedrich von Gentz	*John Quincy Adams*

Note what the following desired at the time of the Treaty of Paris in 1783:

Spain	*France*	*American delegates*

Pic 157: What illicit or rather not so illicit thing is going on in this cartoon?

Varying Viewpoints 158: What did the following historians have to say about the revolution?

George Bancroft	*Beer/Andrews/Gipson*	*Carl Becker/J.F. Jameson*
R. Brown/E. Morgan	*Bernard Bailyn*	*Gary Nash*
Woody Holton	*Fred Anderson*	*David Armitage*

People have the right to have rights. I think.

Quote 161: What does Jefferson believe America can provide a good example of to the world?

_____

The longest-lived constitution in the world is that of the State of	In the British tradition, a 'constitution' was not written, rather, it was:

Articles of Confederation

Pg. 163: Examining the Evidence. What about American history does this item illuminate?

_____

_____

_____

Pic 164: Who are these merchants and what are they doing in this picture?

_____

The Articles of Confederation focused on the   *legislative*   *executive*   *judicial*   branch.

Map 165: What did it mean for a state to 'cede land to the United States?'	Pic 166: Note some of the historic events that took place at Independence Hall, Philadelphia:

Highlight some of the 'weaknesses' of the Articles of Confederation that prompted the founders to think about replacing it:

Old Northwest

Land Ordinance of 1785

Northwest Ordinance

Map 167: Draw a township (left) and a square mile division under L.O. of 1785 (from the insets):

Note how Britain acted against American economic interests in these years- mention Lord Sheffield:	Note how Spain acted against American economic interests in these years:

Map 168: The centers of British and Spanish power in U.S. territory were:

British   *Spanish*

John Jay

Shays' Rebellion

Pic 169: How did the presence of so many people in debt affect national leaders?

Constitutional Convention

'Sword of the Revolution'

'The elder statesman'

'Father of the Constitution'

Alexander Hamilton

Dey of Algiers

Pic 171: Franklin commented on the symbolism of Washington's tall chair. What did he mean?	Describe the characteristics of the 55 legislators :

Virginia Plan

New Jersey Plan

The Great Compromise

House of Representatives

Senate

Common law

Civil law

Electoral College

Three-fifths Compromise

Checks and balances

"We the People"

Pic 173: How long in total hours spent did the Constitution take to draft in 1787? _____

Table 174: What did the Constitution have to say about the following:

Importing more slaves   *Runaway slaves*

Quote 174: What do you think Ben Franklin was implying in his famous answer to the woman who asked him about the kind of government America was to have?

Antifederalists

Federalists

Table 175: In what ways was the Constitution stronger than the Articles of Confederation?

Map 176: Generalize the location of people who were more antifederalist in their beliefs:

Table 176: Why do you think Delaware calls itself "the First State?"

The Federalist

Pic 177: The Society of Pewterers is most like   *a modern cartel*   *a medieval guild*

Pic 178: Draw
and label the
pillars:

The <u>final</u> document is best described as: *radical*   *conservative*   *monarchical*

Contending Voices 179 – What did the following argue concerning the Constitution:

Jonathan Smith   *Patrick Henry*

Who do you agree with more?

Society of the Cincinnati

Disestablishment

Pic 180: Americans love forming groups and societies. What was the point of this one?

_____

_____

Virginia Statute for Religious Freedom

Quotes 179/180: Analyze both these quotes:

	179	*180*

Who said it:

What did they say:

When did they say it:

Where did they say it:

Why did they say it:

Civic virtue

Republican motherhood

Pic 180: What did Elizabeth Mumbet Freeman do?	How is it similar to what the Africans on the island in the quote thought?

Varying Viewpoints 181: How did each historian argue?

John Fiske	*Charles A. Beard*	*Brown & McDonald*
Gordon Wood	*David Waldstreicher*	*Woody Holton*

Federalist: "Everyone come to Washington D.C. for a meeting." Antifederalist: "Let's just Zoom this meeting. Seriously. We don't need to go there."

Quote 184: Based on his quote here, do you think Alexander Hamilton would have advised President George W. Bush to go ahead with the plan to bring American-style democratic government to Iraq in 2003? Why or why not?

The section entitled "Growing Pains" points out that the total population of the United States reached 4 million by 1790. What is the closest metropolitan area to you with a population of over 4 million?

| Quote 184: Robert Turgot was France's top economist of the day. How did he regard the new experiment of America?

| _____

The only president to ever have been elected unanimously was _____

Of the long list of cabinet positions on pg. 185, list the ones that are still the same today, and the ones that are gone or transformed:

The same today

Gone or morphed

Bill of Rights

How do the following guarantee non-enumerated rights to remain with the states and the people:

Ninth Amendment

Tenth Amendment

Judiciary Act of 1789

Pic 186: What does this poster say George Washington is? _____

Funding at par

Assumption

Pic 187: Contrast Jefferson's vision of an ideal America with Hamilton's:

Jefferson   *Hamilton*

Chart 188: How much total debt did the USA have during this time? _____

Tariff

Do the authors of the textbook seem pro-Hamilton or pro-Jefferson? Demonstrate your position using a quote from this section, which may be adjectives use to describe their respective doings:

Excise tax

Pic 190: How do you *know* the cartoonist favors the rebels who opposed Hamilton's tax?

Bank of the United States

Whiskey Rebellion

Quote 191: Which founder, Jefferson or Hamilton, had more confidence in the people of America to take care of themselves without control from above?

| Quote 190: What did Breckenridge say
| about the Whiskey Rebel situation?

Is it strange they don't tell you, student and reader, that foreign interests owned much of the Bank of 'America?' Or that the 'Bank of America' was in fact a private corporation given the right to mint money, just like its descendent, the Federal Reserve Bank (the Fed), does today? If someone asked you to find evidence that the authors of the textbook are very pro-Hamilton and anti-Jefferson, could you find any such evidence on pg. 190-191?

Does the textbook laud or criticize the two-party system? _____

What do you think the authors of the textbook mean when they write, "The party out of power traditionally plays the invaluable role of the balance wheel on the machinery of government"?

_____

Chart 191: Copy the chart to see how the parties currently in power were formed:

_____

French Revolution
_____

Pic 192: Why were some Americans disgusted with the French Revolution?

_____

Thinking Globally 194 – How does this article **compare** _the French Revolution with the American?_

_____

Reign of Terror
_____

Neutrality Proclamation
_____

Anthony Wayne
_____

Battle of Fallen Timbers
_____

Chief Little Turtle
_____

Treaty of Greenville
_____

| Map 196: Which territories that would Become states in the future were added to the U.S. after 1783? | Pic 197: What was the overall consequence of the U.S.-Indian conflicts during this era? |

Jay's Treaty

Pinckney's Treaty

Washington's Farewell Address

What did Washington recommend for the country in the Farewell Address?

Pic 198: Recalling his lucid defense of the Boston Massacre shooters in the British Army, what other pursuits did John Adams have before going for law?

Quote 199: Jefferson's statement indicates God is distant from human affairs. This Corresponds most with (see pg. 309):

Traditional Christianity   deism   atheism

Pic 199: What caused the XYZ Affair?

| The slogan raised against France at this
| time was:
|
|

Pic 200: The *Philadelphia* would see action in the battle against the Barbary Pirates. Look up what country the city of Tripoli, from which they came, is the capital of today:

Convention of 1800

Alien Laws

Sedition Act

Matthew Lyon

Pic 202: What exactly is going on in this picture and why is it happening?

Virginia Resolution

Kentucky Resolution

What did John Jay think about who should govern the United States?
|
|

Copy Table 204, to see the contrast in the political platforms of the following parties:

The Federalists	The Democratic-Republicans
1.	
2.	
3.	
4.	
5.	
6.	
7.	
8.	
9.	
10.	
11.	
12.	
13.	

Pic 204: What did it mean that Jefferson was a "natural bridge?"

Quote 205: What does Jefferson say he wants in this statement?

All that being said, to what extent do you agree or disagree with the Jeffersonian vision of America?

PRESIDENTIAL DOLLARS

Engraver _____

Search: Presidential $1 Coin Program

President name	Term Start	First Lady name	Activity – in one word!
1			
2			
3			
4			
5			
6			
7			
8			
9			
10			
	2nd wife:		
11			
12			
13			
14			
15			
16			
17			
18			
19			
20			
21			
22			

President name	Term Start	First Lady name	Activity – in one word!
23			
24			
25			
26			
27			
28			
	2ⁿᵈ wife:		
29			
30			
31			
32			
33			
34			
35			
36			
37			
38			
39			
40			
41			
42			
43			
44			
45			

Teacher: "From now on there's going to be a property requirement for you to turn in late work." Student: "Huh?"

Quote 210: What do the following mean in Jefferson's statement and beyond:

Despotism   *Boisterous*   *Mudslinging*

_____   _____   _____

Note some of the fire the Federalists came under during this era:

_____

"Whispering campaign"

Quote 210: In France at the time, Jacobin (radicals) were tearing down old Gothic churches and putting up 'temples of wisdom' in their place. When the Rev. Timothy Dwight says American sons will be converted to Voltaire and Marat, he means they will lose religion and become

a. too liberal   b. too moderate   c. too conservative

| Pic 211: How do you know this is a
| *propaganda* image?
|
|_____
|
|_____
|
|_____

Lame Duck

Revolution of 1800

Map 212: Geographically speaking, where were the states that voted against Jefferson located?

Quote 212: Why was this lady so amazed at the way U.S. administration ran?
|
|
|
|

Pg. 213: Examining the Evidence. The first American presidential sex-scandal!

If you were a lawyer trying to accuse Jefferson of being the father of at least some of Sally Hemmings' children, what evidence would you present from this article?

_____

_____

_____

_____

| Hmm... interesting. Now take note:
| 1 – DNA results say a male in the
| Jefferson line was the father of one
| of Sally's many children- Eston. But
| there were 26 male Jeffersons with that
| DNA around her at the time.
|
| 2 – Sally was 14 and accompanied
| Jefferson in Paris as a maid, along with
| his daughters of the same age. Seriously?
| Jefferson was 64 at the time. The
| daughters both denied it too. Now what?
|

Pic 214: The carriage at the foot of the daughter in this picture is said to be attesting to her:

    a. Poverty- it was the only one they had   *b. Wealth and privilege*

Did you have any toys like that-
cars etc. when you were a kid?

    a. Yes   *b. No*

| If there were no cameras all over with people taking
| pics- selfies and otherwise- and you only had one
| shot at a family portrait, what would you wear:
|
| *a. Regular clothes*   *B. your best clothes*

Pic 215: What kind of clothes did Jefferson favor?

_____

Quote 215: What was Kennedy's opinion of T.J.?

We know the polygraph as a lie-detector machine. But what did Jefferson use this one for?

_____

Judiciary Act of 1801 _____

"Midnight Judges" _____

John Marshall _____

Marbury v. Madison _____

Pic 217: John Marshall was   *a. Born into wealth*   *b. A rags-to-riches story*

Jefferson was a war hawk, ready to entangle in international alliances: *a. True*   *b. False*

Barbary states _____

The pashas of North Africa organized the pirates, agents of Muslim states based in these cities:

_____

Map 218: Where did the major battle take place?

_____

| Their 'piracy' was raiding the Spanish, Italian
| and other coasts looking for villagers to capture
| as slaves, and extortion. How did Jefferson
| respond to these states' demands for tribute?
|
|
| _____

Pic 218: Why did the Americans burn their own ship, the *Philadelphia,* as shown here?

_____

Note the results of the Tripolitan War and how it affect the U.S. military and psyche:
Explain the situation in France when Napoleon agreed to sell the Louisiana Territory:

Haitian Revolution

Pic 220: Toussaint led the ex-slaves in the French colony of Saint-Domingue (Haiti) against the French, and killed many before Napoleon had him captured and brought to France. What happened to him then?

| What happened to the colony?

Louisiana Purchase

Corps of Discovery

Lewis & Clark

Sacajawea

Zebulon Pike

Pic 221: Describe the journey of Lewis and Clark:

| Pic 221 (right): Why did Clark refer to
| these Indians as 'flatheads?'

Pic 223: What might be the propaganda value of giving the Indian chiefs of the west these medallions?

| Map 222: Along the border of which
| modern states did Lewis & Clark find the
| Pacific?

Aaron Burr

Why do the authors refer to Britain and France as the 'Tiger and the Shark' in this period?

Orders in Council

Impressment

Chesapeake Affair

Embargo Act of 1807

Pic 225: Why do you think people who live in coastal towns tend to be against embargos?

Contending Voices 229 – Why the different perspectives?

Non-Intercourse Act

Quote 226: What utterly amazing coincidence occurred on July 4, 1826?

| Pic 227: What are the British and French shown doing here?

Macon's Bill #2

Did Madison's gamble work? Why or why not?

Tecumseh

War Hawks

Pic 228: Note the consequences of the battles of the Themes and Tippecanoe:

William Henry Harrison

"Scalp buyers"

Quote 229: This president was an 'Indian fighter':   Quote 228 (right): Is Tecumseh a capitalist?

a. Lyndon Johnson   *b. W.H. Harrison*   *a. Totally*   *b. Not really*

Pic 229: Note the political positions of the following during this time:

Jeffersonians   *Federalists*

In closing, if you could go back in time and talk to Jefferson, would you advise him to purchase Louisiana? Why?

Pg. 232   11 – THE WAR OF 1812 & UPSURGE OF NATIONALISM   Hymnist _____

"You may have to water the tree of liberty every 20 years or so." With what? "Oh nothing, just the blood of patriots and tyrants."

Quote 232: What was James Monroe's message to Europe and Asia in 1823?

War of 1812

From which three places were American troops dispatched for Canada in 1812?

1   *2*   *3*

Rate the action of the American Navy in 1813 as against both the American Army and the British:

"Old Ironsides"

Oliver Hazard Perry

Detroit is the only American city to have surrendered to a foreign force since the independence of the country. Who did it surrender to in the War of 1812?

Map 233: After which battle on Lake Erie did Perry say, "We have me the enemy and they are ours," reinvigorating the American cause?

Map 233: Which large U.S. city was burned to the ground by the British?

Map 233: Before the great Battle of New Orleans, maybe the most famous unnecessary battle in history, where did Jackson fight the Creek Indian Red Sticks?

Pic 234: What did Henry Adams say after the U.S.S. *Constitution* defeated the H.M.S. *Guerriere* at sea?

Thomas Macdonough

Fort McHenry

Francis Scott Key

Star Spangled Banner

The Battle of New Orleans happened   *a. Before*   *b. After*   the war was over.

(Whatever you do, don't Youtube: Battle of New Orleans Johnny Horton and listen to it on loudest volume in the middle of class)

Congress of Vienna

Treaty of Ghent

Quote 235: During the Haitian Revolution a decade earlier, white French soldiers caught malaria and the disease killed more of them than the enemy fighters. Ultimately, they had to withdraw because of it, and it was determined that Europeans should not fight in tropical climes during the summer malarial season. Jackson knew this. What evidence of that is here in this quote?

| Pic 235: What kinds of things did the British promise to states willing to quit the Union and rejoin the British Empire?

Hartford Convention

Quote 237: What was this British lieutenant's opinion of Americans and American soldiers?

| Map 237: In the 1812 election, generalize about the location of the states who voted for Clinton:

While the authors state (231) the War of 1812 was "but a footnote" to the Napoleonic Wars going on in Europe, what did the war do for Americans?

Rush-Bagot Agreement

Pic 238: What does 'rustic' mean in the context of this famous picture of the White House in 1826?

Tariff of 1816

The American System

Pic 240: What kinds of policies might the U.S. government enact today that would be like a modern version of the American System?

James Monroe

Era of Good Feelings

Pic 240 (right): Aside from Old Glory, what other distinctively American symbols are there here?

Quote 241: The message presented here is:

a. Meant to be ironic

b. You are a lucky country America, enjoy while it lasts

Panic of 1819

Some causes of the Panic of 1819 were:

Pic 241: What two bodies of water did the Erie Canal link?

Land Act of 1820

Tallmadge Amendment

The "Peculiar Institution"

Pic 243: Don't read the caption yet! If you saw these silk bags in a museum, with black women doing work and slaves being whipped, which of the following would you think it was at first sight?

a. Racist, pro-slavery propaganda

b. Abolitionist anti-slavery propaganda

Were you right after reading the caption?   a. Yes   b. No

Missouri Compromise

Map 244: What did the North get out of giving up Missouri to the South?

Quote(s) 244: What were the opinions of Jefferson and Adams on slavery and the race issue in America?

John Marshall

Pic 246: Webster's great quote was:
Note the judicial significance of the following cases:

McCulloch v. Maryland

Cohens v. Virginia

Gibbons v. Ogden   *Fletcher v. Peck*

Dartmouth v. Woodward   Quote 240: What was the chief criticism
                                        of John Marshall by the NY Times?

Oregon Country

Anglo-American Convention

Map 247: What year did the U.S.-British | Why do you think what is now Northern Maine was
Treaty Line decide the border between | disputed by the U.S. and Britain?
the U.S. and Canada? |
 |
 |
 |
 |
 (Whatever you do, do NOT do a video search for 'SNL Maine Justice' to see how it was settled)

Map 247 (bot.): Note Jackson's response to | After hanging the two British officials at St.
the Indian raids into Georgia and the | Marks and 'pacifying' the Indians and escaped
Mississippi Territory: | slaves in the interior of Florida, where did
 | Jackson head next to encounter the Spanish?
 |
 |
 |

Adams-Onis Treaty

Pic 248: What did people mean by giving | Why did many feel the world had to be made safe
Jackson the nickname "Old Hickory?" | *from* democracy after the French Revolution?
 |
 |
 |

Russo-American Treaty

Pic 249: Compare the map on Monroe's wall | Quote 250: Why might the Colombian
in the background against the map on pg. 243. | newspaper be more positive about the *Monroe*
What is different about the two? | *Doctrine* than Metternich?
 |
 |
 |

*"I... killed... the bank!" -President Andrew Jackson; his last words before he died, when asked about his **greatest** accomplishment.*

Quote 253: Under what conditions did Jackson argue American people had a right to complain about the injustice of their government?

_____

Corrupt Bargain
_____

Describe the political status of the following:

John Q. Adams

Henry Clay

John C. Calhoun

Andrew Jackson

_____

Pic 254: What does it mean when it says politicians realized they had to "get the message to the man"?

| Jackson was by far the most popular in
| 1824- why didn't he win?
|
|
|
|

_____

Pic 255: J.Q. Adams was the first "Minority President"- what does the term mean?

| Note some of the things Adams did that the
| public didn't like while in office:
|
|
|
|
|

_____

When the nation went "Whole Hog" for Jackson in the mid-1820s after the Corrupt Bargain, what were some of the slogans they used? Which was the catchiest to you?

1)   2)   3)

_____

Map 257: Which candidate | Quotes 257/58: Contrast the three opinions of the polarizing Jackson
did Michigan, Arkansas and |
Florida vote for in 1828? | *Anti-Jackson Newspaper*   *Maryland Supporter*   *Jefferson*
(trick question) |
|

Quote 258: What did Charles Dickens (who wrote *A Christmas Carol* and *A Tale of Two Cities*) think about America's common-man equality?

Spoils system

Thinking Globally 260: "Democracy in America" is one of the great works of American history, and a Frenchman wrote it! He came, he saw, he wrote about the U.S. in its youth. Note three distinctive things he described about the country:

1)   2)   3)

Tariff of Abominations

Protectionism

Quote 262: Why did John C. Calhoun use the term 'union' or 'confederacy' instead of 'nation' when describing the U.S.A.?

Pic 262: South Carolina started the Civil War (at least- it helped trigger the beginning of hostilities) by seceding from the U.S. on December 26, 1860. How many years *before* this event did South Carolina begin *thinking* about seceding?

| Pic 262: Calhoun believed in the Union, but what did he argue was necessary to preserve the Union?

The South Carolina Exposition

Nullification

Do you think a state should be able to nullify a federal law that the state believes is unconstitutional *or* not in its best interests? Why or why not?

| Quote 263: Whose toast would you have cheered most- Jackson's or Calhoun's?

Compromise Tariff of 1833

Force Bill

Pic 264: Today forced separation of one people from another, such as white Americans and Indians, is called ethnic cleansing. What was Jackson's rationale for moving the tribes to reservations out west?

| Describe the steps the Cherokees took to assimilate to white American culture before being removed to reservations anyway:

Pic 264: Out of the fifteen thousand Cherokees that were ethnically cleansed by the U.S. Army, how many actually made it?

| Is ethnic cleansing going on in places in the world today?

Y   N

(Look it up if you don't know!)

Indian Removal Act

Trail of Tears

Black Hawk War

Chief Oceola

Seminole War

Map 265: Name all the tribes that were forcibly relocated west to Indian Territory:

| Pic 265: Is Black Hawk or his son more assimilated to American ways?

| Many U.S. sports teams are names after Indian-related themes. Chicago's hockey team is the Blackhawks, named for the chief shown here. Do you think this is offensive or does it do honor to the man?

Bank of the United States

What made 'The Bank' a 'moneyed monster' in Jackson's eyes? | 'The Bank' was:

a. A government institution
b. A private company

Nicholas Biddle

The Bank War

| How did Clay try to use 'The Bank' to surefire win the next election against Jackson? | How did Jackson shock the government in response? |

Jackson was shot by an assassin but survived, and blamed international banking interests for hiring the killer. He called 'The Bank' a 'many-headed hydra' too, but even more seriously, what famous quote did he speak, notifying privately what he would do to 'The Bank' in return?

Quote 267: It is   *likely*   *unlikely*   that Biddle really was "delighted" with Jackson's veto.

Pic 268: What are the following doing in this comic, and what does it mean?

The Pro-Bank Men   *Biddle*   *Jackson*

Literally:

Meaning:

Anti-Masonic party

| On a 1-10 scale, how much credence do you give to conspiracy theories about the Illuminati, the Mason, the Rothschild bankers etc.? | Pic 269: What sly move does Jackson use to disarm Biddle in the fight for 'The Bank?' |

Biddle's Panic

Pet banks

Specie Circular

Martin Van Buren

MVB was a man of many nicknames. Provide four of them, and judge whether it has a positive or negative connotation:

1   *3*

2   *4*

Pg. 271: Examining the Evidence. What about American history does this item illuminate?

Panic of 1837

Pic 272: Why didn't anyone relish getting a 'Long Bill'? | Quote 272: Why is a bank run a
                                                             | economically dangerous thing?
                                                             |
                                                             |
                                                             |
                                                             |

Davy Crockett

Jim Bowie

Sam Houston

Steve Austin

Note the development of events during the following years in Texas:

1821:   1833:

1823:   1835:

1830:   1836:

Pic 273: The leader and hero of the Texas rebels was: The message of the Texans was:

Santa Anna

Battle of the Alamo

Battle of Goliad

Battle of San Jacinto

Pic 274 (bot.): Why did the Alamo become a | Map 275: What was strategic about Houston's
rallying cry for the Texas and the Americans? | retreat toward the United States?
                                               |
                                               |
                                               |

Why do you think the Americans help the Texans at crucial moments during the Texas Revolution?

_____

Okay one last nickname for Martin van Buren: _____

Pg. 276: What are some of the things the Anglo 'Texicans' did to become 'Makers of America'?

_____

_____

_____

"Old Tippecanoe" _____

John Tyler _____

Pic 278: Why did Harrison and Tyler have these 'kerchiefs' made for women- when women couldn't vote?	What role did log cabins and hard cider play in this election?

Pic 279: Explain what is happening to Van Buren:

On the Left   *On the Right*

Do you think all presidents go through something like this? Why or why not?

Two-Party System _____

Relate the status of the two national parties after 1840:

The Democrats (Differences)	Similarities	The Whigs (Differences)

Pic 280: Is this painting a good reflection on the age? Why or why not?

Quote 280: Jackson's advice as to how to know a Democrat from a Whig said one should...

Pg. 281: Varying Viewpoints. What did the following historians have to say about Jacksonian democracy?

Frederick Jackson Turner

Arthur Schlesinger

Richard Hofstadter

Marvin Meyers

Lee Benson

Sean Wilentz

Charles Sellers

Daniel Walker How

Which do you agree with most?

13 – FORGING THE NATIONAL ECONOMY **Know-Something**_____

Provide your answers in Morse Code for extra credit* *At U.S. Military Academy only*

Quote 284: Emerson believes the advancement of new technologies | Emerson also believes

a. *bolsters established governments* b. *diffuses central power* | a. *America is stodgy & old*

The American West was a. *tough* b. *full of opportunities* c. *both* | b. *America is vital & new*

Self-reliance _____

Rendezvous _____

Ecological imperialism _____

Map 285: Note the year the center of American population passed the following cities:

_____ *Washington, D.C.* _____ *Pittsburgh, PA* _____ *Cleveland, OH*

_____ *Cincinnati, OH* _____ *Chicago, IL* _____ *St. Louis, MO*

Pic 286: What evidence do we have here that European noblemen were fascinated with the rugged American West? | What evidence do we have that | the West was sometimes a little | too rugged?

Note some big-city problems that appeared due to rapid urbanization in the mid-19th century:

Graph 287: Describe the general pattern of growth by race leading up to 1860: | Alright math nerds, figure this one out. Given that | during the Civil War in the 1860s a total of 580,000 | whites died and 40,000 nonwhites, did the trend | continue in *that* decade? Show your work ;)

Graph 287 (bot.): *Which decade did the most Irish people immigrate to America?*_____

*Which decade did the most German people immigrate to America?*_____

Quote 288: Describe two kinds of people coming to America from Germany in the 19th century:

Pic 288: The 19th century's equivalent of widescreen TV, describe the uniquely American reasons artists chose the aesthetic shown here:

_____

There were more Irish-Americans by the end of the 19th century than there were Irish: *T   F*

Ancient Order of Hibernians
_____

Molly Maguires
_____

Tammany Hall
_____

Quote 289: What kind of advice did Margaret McCarthy write to her relatives in Ireland?

_____

48ers
_____

Kindergarten
_____

Pg. 290: What are some of the things the Irish did to become 'Makers of America'?

_____

_____

_____

Pic 292: This cartoon implies two things about the Irish and Germans. What are they?

1)   *2)*

_____

Know-Nothing party
_____

Awful Disclosures
_____

Nativists
_____

Industrial Revolution
_____

"Voices" 293: The Know-Nothing platform said: | Transcendentalist Orestes Brownson said:

Samuel Slater _____

Textiles _____

Eli Whitney _____

Cotton gin _____

Pg. 291: What are some of the things the Germans did to become 'Makers of America'?

_____

_____

Pic 294: What did this factory mill produce? | Describe the rise and fall of the early mills between the years 1807 and 1816:

Samuel Colt _____

Patent Office _____

Pic 295: How did the cotton gin affect plantation life and slavery as a labor system?

_____

_____

Limited liability _____

Samuel Morse _____

Charles Goodyear _____

Quote 296: _____ remains the only president ever to have obtained a patent.

Quote 297: What does the term 'wage slavery' mean in the context of industrial workers in New England?

| Besides European indentured servants and African slaves, companies used white children to do these kinds of jobs:

'Scabs' and 'rats' _____

Commonwealth v. Hunt _____

Pic 297: Which job would you rather have, the one on the right or the left? Why?

_____

_____

Pg. 298: Examining the Evidence. What about American history does this item illuminate?

_____

_____

Factory girls _____

Cult of domesticity _____

Pic 300: Would you have rather been a girl who worked in a factory or mill as in this picture, or have been a homemaker? Why?

_____

Pic 301: How do you know the black woman in this picture is employed by the household and not a slave?	Where was McCormick's factory located?

McCormick reaper _____

Pic 302: What do you think was the general level of sound working at this factory? _____

Turnpike _____

Robert Fulton _____

Clermont _____

Pic 303: Would you have rather been a passenger on one of the boats pictured or on the *Sultana*? Why?

_____

Erie Canal _____

The Iron Horse _____

Map 304: In order to get by boat from New York City to Detroit, one can take the

_____

to Albany, followed by the

_____

to Buffalo, followed by

_____

to Detroit.

'Sleeping Palace'

_____

George Pullman

_____

Clipper ships

_____

Map 309: Before the Civil War, the Pony Express carried mail from Salt Lake City to San Francisco:

  a. True   *b. False*

Pony Express

_____

Transportation revolution

_____

Market revolution

_____

One could get from Chicago to Indianapolis by road in this era:

  a. True   *b. False*

It was possible to get from New York City to New Orleans by boat stopping at Chicago on the way:

  a. True   *b. False*

Map 301: The densest area of the country for railroad lines was:
  a. the industrial north   *b. the agrarian south*

Mark Twain implied the coach trip to California was very:

  a. Mountainous and difficult *b. Easy*

Describe how the economic climate changed under Chief Justice Roger Taney:

Map 309: Note the states that specialized in the following:

Flour mills:

Textile mills:

Shoes/clothes:

Iron and steel:

Map 309: Note the states that had the following resources:

Silver and gold:

Copper:

Iron:

Coal:

Map 309: Note the states that specialized in the following agricultural products:

Corn and wheat: *Dairy and hay:*

Tobacco and hemp: *Cotton, rice and sugarcane:*

Map 309: Note the states that specialized in the following products:

Range and ranch cattle:

Orchard fruits:

Lumber and timber:

John Jacob Astor

'Drifters'

'Rags to riches' story

Pic 310: Chicago was laid out in a   *a. regular grid*   *b. irregular natural*   pattern.

Timeline 311: What kind of invention did John Deere have before getting into the tractor business?	Under President Van Buren, federal workers began working this many hours:

London's great fair that displayed all the new inventions of the age was held in _____

What did Howe and Singer invent?	What did Cyrus Field accomplish?

Pg. 313   14 – FERMENT OF REFORM AND CULTURE   Transcendentalist_____

No, you are not allowed to Missouri Compromise your way out of doing half this assignment.

Quote 313: This Emerson quote is about: *a. Growing up*   *b. America*   *c. Both*

The Age of Reason

Deism

After examining the Tocqueville quote and the bases of deism on pg. 313, summarize how America's religiosity was changing in the mid-19th century:

_____

_____

Second Great Awakening

Pic 314: How is a revival such as this one different than a traditional church service? | Pic 315: Name three things Charles Finney argued would help bring society closer to recreating God's heavenly kingdom on earth:

Burned-Over District

Joseph Smith

Mormons

Pic 316: The Mormon trek west is most like the video game: | Map 317: The Mormons followed this natural feature much of the way to Utah:

a. Oregon Trail   *b. Minesweeper*   *c. GTA 7*

Brigham Young

Quote 317: What is polygamy, as it is referred to in this statement? | What years did Congress pass anti-polygamy laws?

Pic 318: If you were a lawyer arguing both sides of this question, what would your main arguments be?

Public education like this schoolhouse is free   *Public education is not really free*

Complete the famous Thomas Jefferson quote:

"A civilized nation that was both ignorant and free...   "

Horace Mann _____

Noah Webster _____

William McGuffey _____

Emma Willard _____

Quote 319: After reading the two quote about education on this page, first by Lincoln and next by Sarah Hale, argue whether they agree or disagree and why:	Pic 320: How had opportunities for women in higher education changed between 1837 and 1872?

Lyceum _____

Godey's Lady's Book _____

Quote 320: What did Dorothea Dix find troubling about the way the mentally ill were being treated?	Pic 321: What did Ms. Dix argue would be a better way to treat people in jail?

Pic 322: Note some of the negative things happening in America due to heavy drinking:

_____

American Temperance Society _____

Ten Nights in a Barroom _____

Maine Law _____

Pic 323: If you were a lawyer arguing both sides of this question, what would your main arguments be?

        Women have it pretty good   *Women are the 'Submerged sex'*

Elizabeth Cady Stanton

Susan B. Anthony

Pic 324: Do you agree with the statement that this image doesn't seem absurd today? Why or why not?

| Quote 324: What do these wedding
| vows mean in layman's (or layperson's)
| terms?
|
|
|
|
|

Seneca Falls

Pg. 325: Examining the Evidence. How can clothes be a symbol of social reform?

New Harmony

Brook Farm

Oneida Community

Shakers

If you could go back in time, which of these four communities would you most want to join?

Contending Voices 326 - Summarize the views of the following:

Seneca Falls writer   *Reform newspaper*
                                |
                                |
                                |
                                |
                                |

With whom do you agree more?

Pic 327 (top): The Shakers are best described as:　　　*a. Hard working*　　　　*b. Lazy*

Note the achievements of the following American scientists:

Nathanial Bowditch　　　　*Matthew Maury*　　　　*Benjamin Silliman*

Louis Agassiz　　　　*Asa Gray*　　　　*John Audubon*

Pg. 328: What are some of the things the Oneidans did to become 'Makers of America'?

_____

_____

_____

Some nasty medical conditions people complained about in the mid-19th century (before the germ theory of disease gained prevalence) were:	Name three common remedies practiced back then that you would totally not use: 1) 2) 3)

Federal style _____

Greek-Revival _____

Monticello _____

Pic 331: Thomas Jefferson's favorite style to design buildings in was _____

Note the kind of art produced by the following:

Gilbert Stuart　　　　*Charles W. Peale*　　　　*John Trumbull*

_____

Hudson River School _____

Thomas Cole _____

Albert Bierstadt _____

Louis Daguerre

Minstrel shows

What would your English teacher say is ironic about the origin of the famous Southern songs *Dixie, Camptown Races, Old Folks at Home* and *Oh! Susanna*?	While the British made fun of American writing, these nonfiction books stood out:

Romanticism

Pic 332: What elements in this painting make it a masterpiece of the Romantic style?

Match the fiction writer with their famous works:

Washington Irving:

James Fennimore Cooper:

William Cullen Bryant:

Transcendentalism

What did the Transcendentalists believe?

Pic 334: If you had to read a book by one of the authors pictured here, who would it be?

The American Scholar

Note the contributions of the following Transcendentalist writers:

Ralph Waldo Emerson   *Henry David Thoreau*

Margaret Fuller   *Walt Whitman*

Quote 335: After reading both of these quotes, answer the question: "Henry D. Thoreau would":

a. Argue you are a good citizen when you do what you are told and are nonviolent
b. Argue you are a good citizen when you do what you think is right violently
c. Argue you are a good citizen when you do what you are told and are violent about it
d. Argue you are a good citizen when you do what you think is right and are nonviolent

Note the contributions of the following 'literary lights':

H.W. Longfellow   *John G. Whittier*

James Russell Lowell   *Louisa May Alcott*

Emily Dickinson   *William Gilmore Simms*

Note the contributions of the following 'dissenting' writers and 'portrayers of the past':

Edgar Allan Poe   *Nathanial Hawthorne*

Herman Melville   *George Bancroft*

William Prescott   *Francis Parkman*

What about these historians was suspect to Southerners?   Pic 338: Would you work in whaling?

Viewpoints 339: What did these historians argue about the 19th century women's movement?

Michael Katz   *B. Quarles & J.B. Stewart*   *Cott, Sklar & Ryan*

C.S. Rosenberg   *N. Hewitt & L. Ginzberg*   *Ellen DuBois*

Romanticism in art had a few key themes you will be able to see in the paintings. The revolutionary upheavals acted as a counterbalance to the reasonableness and logic of the Enlightenment era. It was a time when feelings ran wild, feelings about nation, about nature and its raw power and beauty, about the past (think fairy tales and being nostalgic about things in your own life), innocence, and all this was channeled through the imagination. Transcending the here and now by following a romantic vision and mission- is what heroes are made of.

Image search: *Artist's Name + Painting's Name*

Artist	Painting	What is going on? / Theme	Rate it (1-10)!
Thomas Cole	Departure	_____	__
Thomas Cole	Return	_____	__
Thomas Cole	A Home in the Woods	_____	__
Thomas Cole	Last of the Mohicans	_____	__
Thomas Cole	Niagara Falls	_____	__
Thomas Cole	The Oxbow River	_____	__
Thomas Cole	View of the Catskills	_____	__
Albert Bierstadt	Light in the Forest	_____	__
Albert Bierstadt	California Spring	_____	__
Albert Bierstadt	Civil Guerrilla Warfare	_____	__
Albert Bierstadt	Mt. Adams, Washington	_____	__
Albert Bierstadt	Mt. Cororan	_____	__
Albert Bierstadt	The Rocky Mountains	_____	__
Albert Bierstadt	Rocky Mountain Storm	_____	__
Albert Bierstadt	Rocky Mountain Tribe	_____	__
Albert Bierstadt	The Sierra Nevadas	_____	__
Albert Bierstadt	Yosemite	_____	__
Frederic Edwin Church	River of Light banner	_____	__
John Frederic Kenset	Eaton's Neck, Long Island	_____	__

Wait, so that was all real?

Quote 342: Lincoln's warning seems to advocate:

    a. Ending slavery because it is in everyone's best interest   *b. Denying freedom to all*

'King Cotton'

Why could the Antebellum South be called a political oligarchy instead of a democracy?	Why did so many Southerners love the novels of Sir Walter Scott?

Pic 344: The cotton bales in this picture are in the city of

_____ headed for _____

What kinds of items manufactured in the North agitated many Southerners because it reminded them of dependence?

| Pic 344: What are the slave workers doing in this picture? _____

Graph 345: The fewest number of slaveowning families owned | The great majority of Southern
_____ slaves, the most owned _____. | whites owned _____ slaves.

This was not an insult that was applied to poor whites in the old South:

    a. poor white trash   *b. ninjas*   *c. crackers*   *d. hillbillies*

Maps 346: In general, the distribution of Southern cotton production between 1820 and 1860:

    a. moved north by northwest   *b. moved west by southwest*   *c. did not move*

Maps 346: This state did not have any counties containing over 50 percent slaves in 1860:

    a. Georgia   *b. South Carolina*   *c. North Carolina*   *d. Virginia*   *e. Missouri*

William T. Johnson

What kinds of social rules existed for the 'Third Race' of free blacks in the South?

Frederick Douglass

West Africa Squadron

Pic 348: Most slaves caught in the Congo were sent to Brazil or the Caribbean. Congo is in:

a. North Africa   b. Central Africa

c. West Africa   d. Southern Africa

| Why were Irish laborers more likely to be hired for dangerous jobs by Southern planters than having slaves undertake them?

Quote 349: Locate three grammar or spelling errors in this letter by Maria Perkins:

Uncle Tom's Cabin

Pic 350: Aside from the slaves being sold at the action depicted on the sign, what other products were being sold alongside the human chattel?

Breakers

Note two incentives planters had not to visit much flogging upon their slaves:

| Pic 351: Why is the slave woman wearing this bizarre collar?

Black belt

Responsorial preaching

Pic 352: Why do you think the planters entrusted 'mammies' with their kids on such a wide scale?

'Peculiar institution'

Nat Turner's Rebellion

Amistad

Pic 353: Which direction are these slaves marching if they are marching to *Tennessee*?

| Why did Southern whites argue they were in a 'state of siege?'

Map 353: Note the states and territories by year they abolished slavery: | Pic 352: What was
                                                                                | this 'box' used for?
                                                                                |
                                                                                |
                                                                                |

American Colonization Society

Republic of Liberia

Monrovia

Quotes 355: Summarize Sojourner Truth's | Summarize the perspective presented at the
perspective on the status of slavery's | American Anti-Slavery Society meeting led
overall situation: | by W.H. Garrison:
                                                 |
                                                 |
                                                 |
                                                 |
                                                 |

Why didn't most African slaves want to go back to Africa when the Colonization Society began its transports?

The Liberator

William Lloyd Garrison

American Anti-Slavery Society

Appeal to the Colored Citizens of the World

Sojourner Truth

Narrative of the Life of Frederick Douglass

Pg. 356: Examining the Evidence. What about American history does this map illuminate?

Pic 357: Where was Frederick Douglass posted at the end of his career?

Mason-Dixon Line

Thinking Globally 358 – Categorize the countries by world region and the year they abolished slavery

Americas   Europe   Middle East   Asia

William Wilburforce

Summarize the pro-slavery argument regarding how comparatively bad Northern 'wage slaves' had it versus the more caring life of the Southern plantation:

| Pic 358: Do these pictures support or go against the idea that northern industrial work was worse than slavery?

Gag Resolution

Varying Viewpoints 361: What did the following historians have to say about slavery?

Ulrich Bonnell Phillips   Frank Tannenbaum   Stanley Elkins

Eugene Genovese   Kenneth Stampp   Lawrence Levine

Blassingame & Gutman   Walter Johnson   Genovese, Jones & Morgan

Philip D. Morgan   Ira Berlin   David Brion Davis

You must transcend the limitations of your mind and become one with the stream of history, for as a river flows, so flows the river of time. -Yoda

Quote 366: By what right- as in by what guiding force- does John O'Sullivan believe Americans are destined to rule the continent from sea to shining sea?

| What happened to President W.H. Harrison a month after taking office, who did *not* benefit from this tragedy, and why?

"Tyler Too"

One of the first things Clay and his Whig allies tried to get Tyler to do was to ascent to a new national bank- like the one Jackson killed. What happened?

"Fiscal Corporation"

"His Accidency"

Tariff of 1842

"Third War with England"

Caroline

Creole

Pic 368: Look closely at the words and the picture. How were the British characterizing the U.S.?

In words: *In picture:*

Aroostook War

Map 369: If you were one of the delegates deciding on the Maine-Canada boundary, judging by the map what do you think the most natural lines would be?

Lone Star Republic

Summarize the foreign powers facing Texas in the run-up to 1840:

Summarize the perspectives on Texas held by the following:

James K. Polk   Henry Clay   John Tyler

_____

Pic 370: Compare this with the picture on pg. 316:

Similarities   *Differences*

_____

| Quote 370: What arguments did Brigadier Green have for supporting the Lone Star Republic? | When the authors write, "Americans were in a 'lick all creation' mood," what did they mean? |

Oregon Country
_____

If you were a lawyer arguing the case, what would your main points be supporting the followings claims upon Oregon Country

Britain	*Russia*	*USA*	*Indian tribes*

Pic 370: Was the trip from St. Louis out west difficult, according to the asterisked note at the bottom of the next page?

_____

Manifest Destiny
_____

54-40 or Fight
_____

The "Dark Horse"
_____

Pic 373: This celebration of | If you were a lawyer arguing both sides, what would your main
the white European settlers | arguments be:
of North America and their |
unstoppable march over the| *Remove this painting*   *Keep it up where it is*
entire continent can still be |
seen in this public building: |
                           |
                           |
                           |

The "Mandate"

Walker Tariff

What were the things on President Polk's *Must List*?

1ˢᵗ

2ⁿᵈ

3ʳᵈ

4ᵗʰ

Map 374: If you were deciding on the best place for a boundary for Oregon, what would you argue
is most logical according to the map?

Pic 375: When was this fort | What three population groups lived in California in 1845?
handed over to the Americans? |
                           |
                           |
                           |

John Slidell

Slidell mission

Zachary Taylor

When Mexican soldiers (allegedly) crossed | When Americans sang, "Ho for the Halls of
the Rio Grande, how did Polk respond? | Montezuma," what did they mean?
                           |
                           |

Spot resolutions

Why were the Mexicans 'spoiling' to fight the Americans in turn?

Stephen W. Kearney

John C. Fremont

Bear Flag Republic

Winfield Scott

Map 377: The "disputed area," according to the map key, is what is now:

    a. Arizona   *b. New Mexico*   *c. Eastern Texas*   *d. Western Texas*

This June 14, 1845 event signaled the independence of California: _____

The first major battle of the Mexican-American War was at Monterrey in September of _____

While Kearny proceeded to Santa Fe and El Paso, winning the battles of _____

and _____ in December 1846, Mexico won its greatest victory of the war near

San Diego at _____. To reinforce the American claim over California and

support Fremont, Commodore John D. _____ left Mazatlan by sea for Monterey.

On land, Mexico's major resistance was defeated at the Battle of Buena Vista in February _____.

General Winfield Scott was dispatched from _____, landed at _____,

fought the Battle of Tampico in _____ and then bounced to _____

by sea before moving inland past Cerro Gordo to _____, where the war was

won in September of _____.

Nicholas Trist

Describe Trist's mission and what came of it:

Treaty of Guadalupe Hidalgo

"Conscience Whigs"

Contending Voices 378 - Summarize the views of the following:

New York Evening Post   Henry Clay

With whom do you agree more?

How did the 'Anglo-Saxon spirit of fair play factor into the treaty? | Pic 379: This guy is most likely saying,
|
| a. Unemployment just went down half a percent!
|
| b. Dude, Scott just raised the Stars and Stripes over Mexico City!
|

The area ceded to the U.S. in the Treaty of Guadeloupe Hidalgo was Spanish territory for 282 years, Mexican territory for 26 years, and American territory for 173 years (as of 2021). To what extent do you think "long-memoried Mexicans" are right to view the U.S. as a "greedy bully?"

Pg. 379: What are some of the things the Californios did to become 'Makers of America?'

Wilmot Proviso

Why did Calhoun refer to Mexico as "forbidden fruit?" | Pic 382: Which soldier here would later
| be famous in the Civil War?
|
|
|
|

50 STATE QUARTERS

Web search: Wikipedia 50 State Quarters

Engraver _____

STATE	YEAR OF STATEHOOD	COIN 'MOTTO' or TOPIC	DESIGN 1-3 (3 = Good)
1. Delaware	1787	"The First State"	
2. Pennsylvania			
3. **New Jersey**			
4. Georgia			
5. Connecticut			
6. Massachusetts			
7. **Maryland**			
8. South Carolina			
9. New Hampshire			
10. Virginia			
11. New York			
12. North Carolina			
13. **Rhode Island**			
14. VERMONT			
15. Kentucky			
16. TENNESSEE			
17. Ohio			
18. Louisiana			
19. Indiana			
20. Mississippi			
21. **Illinois**			
22. **Alabama**			
23. MAINE			
24. **Missouri**			

25. Arkansas _____ _____ _____

26. Michigan _____ _____ _____

27. Florida _____ _____ _____

28. Texas _____ _____ _____

29. Iowa _____ _____ _____

30. Wisconsin _____ _____ _____

31. California _____ _____ _____

32. Minnesota _____ _____ _____

33. Oregon _____ _____ _____

34. Kansas _____ _____ _____

35. West Virginia _____ _____ _____

36. NEVADA _____ _____ _____

27. Nebraska _____ _____ _____

38. Colorado _____ _____ _____

39. North Dakota _____ _____ _____

40. SOUTH DAKOTA _____ _____ _____

41. Montana _____ _____ _____

42. Washington _____ _____ _____

43. Idaho _____ _____ _____

44. Wyoming _____ _____ _____

45. Utah _____ _____ _____

46. Oklahoma _____ _____ _____

47. New Mexico _____ _____ _____

48. Arizona _____ _____ _____

49. Alaska _____ _____ _____

50. Hawaii _____ _____ _____

Quote 385: Webster warns here that: | What did politicians fear if the two political parties
                                          | became 'sectional'?

    a. 1776 will not be repeated

    b. Easy come, easy go

Popular sovereignty

Are you a true democrat in the Rousseauean sense (look up 'General Will of the People') and support the *idea* of popular sovereignty? Or do you think a greater force should prevail over the wishes of 'the people' when a moral issue you find offensive is at stake?

'Taylor fever'

Pic 386: When the U.S. invaded Iraq in 2003, many commentators around the world portrayed President Bush's popularity in the 2004 election in a way that was similar to this picture of Zachary Taylor. Many also portrayed President Obama this way when he was awarded the Nobel Peace Prize despite continuing war policies. In your opinion, should political leaders be subjected to this kind of scrutiny by the media, or should the media form less of an opposition and propagandize for the policies of the established politicians?

Free Soil Party

In what ways did the Free Soil Party reach out to disaffected members of the other parties?

Sutter's Mill

Gold Rush

Quote 387: Not only men went out west to Cali in '49, what kinds of 'sly women' did as well?

Map 387: Gold Rush territory was in the   *a. South*   *b. Center*   *c. North*   of California.

The Gold Mines had funny or offensive names at times. Look them up and categorize them into…

Named after places   *Named after people(s)*   *Named after verbs & adjectives*

Pic 388: In this picture, what is the process by which the gold is separated from the ore?

Underground Railroad

Pic 389: If it wasn't a literal railroad, why did they call it one?

| Pic 390: Name the famous woman who was a
| leading 'stationmaster' on the Underground:
| Railroad
|
|

Map 389: What was Texas' claim to the land shown here?

| Was slavery ever allowed in
| Washington DC?
|
|

Summarize the 'twilight' moves of the three 'Senatorial Giants':

Henry Clay   *John C. Calhoun*   *Daniel Webster*   *Ralph Waldo Emerson*
(Quote 391)

7th of March Speech

William Seward

Compromise of 1850

Chart 392: Note what the following got out of the Compromise:

The North   *The South*

Pic 392: What symbols can you find that suggest the artist approved of Clay's work as much as the Senators did?

Fugitive Slave Law

Pic 394: How can you tell this cartoon was done by someone sympathetic to abolition?

Map 395: The territories not opened to slavery included:

The territories that were open to slavery included:

How many representatives did the free states have? _____ Slave states? _____

Map 395: What year did your state abolish slavery? (If you live in the Old South, it's 1865): _____

Contending Voices 396 - Summarize the views of the following:

John C. Calhoun   *Daniel Webster*

|
|
|
|
|
|

With whom do you agree more?

Millard Fillmore

Note the charges the Whigs laid on Franklin Pierce:	How did the Democrats respond?	Why did Scott lose in '52?

What was going on that led up to the Clayton-Bulwer Treaty?	Map 397: How many years would it be from 1850 to the year the U.S. acquired access to build the Panama Canal?

Ostend Manifesto

Opium War

Treaty of Wanghia _____

"Most favored nation" status _____

"Extraterritoriality" _____

Matthew C. Perry _____

Treaty of Kanagawa _____

Pic 399: What evidence in the painting is there of the 'vivid impression' the gift from Perry made on this Japanese artist?

Gadsden Purchase _____

What was Jefferson Davis' rationale for sending Gadsden to make this offer to Mexico?	Had Mexico not agreed to sell the Gadsden land, this large city would likely not be American:

Stephen Douglas _____

Kansas-Nebraska Act _____

Map 400: The Union-Pacific Railroad runs through the current states of:

Pic 397: What was Douglas' rationale for forwarding the Kansas-Nebraska Act?

Republican Party _____

Quote 402: Sumner described the Kansas-Nebraska Act as:

What was his rationale for the following: _____

Why it was 'the worst'   *Why it was 'the best'*

"You know Toto, I don't think we're in Bleedin' Kansas anymore."

Quote 404: In your opinion, are there any issues today in America that bring to mind this quote by Lincoln, that a "House divided against itself cannot stand?"

_____

Uncle Tom's Cabin

Pic 405: What did Lincoln say to Harriet Beecher Stowe upon meeting her? | Pic 405 (r.): Why did Southerners say she didn't "know what she was talking about?"

Quote 404: What is the name of the brutal character in the novel? _____

Hinton Helper

Impending Crisis of the South

Pg. 406: Examining the Evidence. What sentimental value does the cabin represent in this passage?

_____

New England Aid Company

Would you have been more swayed by the call of Whittier's song about making the west the homestead of the free, or the appeal to giving Southern rights to all that was a rejoinder?

_____

Lecompton Constitution

James Buchanan

Bleeding Kansas

Map 407: List the battles in Kansas in order of when they happened:

Pic 408: By what actions did John Brown 'besmirch' the free soil cause?

_____

Pic 409: Who is beating down who here, and where?

Who: *Where:*   *Why:*

_____

Quote 409: How did the following view the beat down:

   Illinois State Journal   *Petersburg Intelligencer*

_____

Map 411: Who finally won this election by | Who did <u>your</u> state vote for in 1856?
carrying the Southland and a few Northern states? |
                                               |
                                               |
                                               |

Dred Scott v. Stanford
_____

Pic 412: Explain the famous- or infamous- Dred Scott case:

   Background: *Legal issue at hand:*   *Verdict:*

_____

Quote 412: What did Chief Justice Roger Taney of the Supreme Court give as an explanation for the decision in the case?

_____

Panic of 1857
_____

Tariff of 1857
_____

Quote 413: During the 2016 & 2020 elections, businessman Donald Trump | Pic 414: What was
& socialist Bernie Sanders both advocated for high protective tariffs, as a | Lincoln's job in his
way to bring jobs back to the United States from cheaper overseas labor | 30s?
markets. Would Lincoln have agreed with their stance on this? |
                                                                          |
                    a. Yes   *b. No*

<u>Lincoln-Douglas debates</u>
_____

<u>Freeport Doctrine</u>
_____

Pic 415: This was the first debate to be shown on TV:

a. True   b. False

| Quote 415: If a (white) presidential candidate said this today, what do you think the reaction would be?

Harpers Ferry

Contending Voices 416 - Summarize the views of the following:

Harriet Tubman   Abraham Lincoln

With whom do you agree more?

Pic 417: At the end when he was going to hang, John Brown   a. Was at peace   b. Was irate

Constitutional Union Party

Pic 418: The first president to play the new game of baseball was:

Chart 418: Did the election of the rail splitter ultimately split the Union?   a. Yes   b. No

Map 419: In which Southern state did all the counties voted for the same candidate?

| What does it mean that Lincoln was a 'minority' president?

Quote 420: What was the Crittenden Compromise and why did it fail?

| Map 420: Which states voted by county unanimously for secession?

Confederate States of America

Jefferson Davis

Pic 421: The look of President Davis of the Confederacy seems: a. Serious   b. Frivolous

Quote 421: What was South Carolina's rationale for secession from the United States?

Moral: Legal:

_____

Quote 422: Did Lincoln follow Greeley's advice presented here?

_____

Pic 423: Did Lincoln follow the American Eagle's advice presented here?

_____

In his message to his congress, what did Jefferson Davis ask of the North?	By world standards, was the South all that different than other nationalist movements in the 1860s?

Quote 423 (right): How did the British view the Southern move to independence?	Do you agree with the parallels between the justification the colonists gave in '76 and what the Southerners gave in 1860?

Why did the parallels 'run even deeper'?

_____

Varying Viewpoints 424: What did the following historians have to say about the Civil War?

Nationalist School   Charles & Mary Beard   J. Randall & A. Craven

A. Nevins & D. Potter   E. Foner & E. Genovese   Ashworth & Lightner

Michael Holt   With whom do you agree most?

_____

What's so civil about war anyway? –Guns n' Roses

Quote 427: Which minority group did Lincoln have in mind in this quote?

| What was symbolic about the way the Capitol dome looked when Lincoln was sworn in?

Was there a significant or logical natural border between the Federal territories and the Confederacy?

| Quote 427 (bot.): Why did Seward propose this half-joke scheme?

How did European powers such as Britain, France, Spain and others stand to *gain* from the U.S. Civil War?

| Pic 428: In which state (or former state) did the first shots of Civil War ring out?

Fort Sumter _____

Note the incidents that took place in these heady opening days of the war:

April 12   *April 15*   *April 19*

Map 429: Note the following:

States that seceded before Fort Sumter	*States that seceded after*	*Slave states loyal to Union*
1	8	1
2	9	2
3	10	3
4	11	4
5		
6		
7		

Border States _____

West Virginia _____

How did Lincoln 'deal' with the Border States? | Quote 429: How did Lincoln feel about
| Kentucky?
|
|
|

Which side did the Indian tribes of Oklahoma favor, and why? | Give an example of a family
| whose members fought on
| opposite sides of the war:
|
|
|

Contending Voices 430 - Summarize the views of the following:

Horace Greeley   *Abe Lincoln*

|
|
|
|
|
|

With whom do you agree more?

Pic 431: Why are these two men 'friendly enemies?'

Robert E. Lee

Thomas Stonewall Jackson

"Yeeeahhh!"

Chart 431: Divide the stats for the Southern states by the Total at bottom, and list the percentage of what the South had vis-à-vis the North:

Manufacturing establishments   *Capital invested*   *Laborers*   *Value of Products*

Pg. 432: What are some of the things 'Billy Yank' and 'Johnny Reb' did to become 'Makers of America'?

Pic 434: What were some of the new technologies deployed in the Civil War?

_____

Ulysses S. Grant
_____

Quote 435: Which side did most British commoners sympathize with according to the American minister?

| Why didn't the South get the foreign
| help it counted on during the Civil War?
|
|
|
|

Pic 435: Which four ethnic immigrants did this poster target? (Look closely, this is a test of your language skills!)

| From what other sources did
| Britain gain the cotton fibers it
| needed for its textile industry?
|
|

Pic 436: What does this cartoon have to do with "Old King Cotton's dead and buried; brave young Corn is King?

_____

Trent Affair
_____

Alabama
_____

Laird rams
_____

Dominion of Canada
_____

Jefferson Davis
_____

Writ of habeas corpus
_____

Pic 438: What is distinctive about the way Abe Lincoln dressed?

| Pic 439: The chances that
| an amputee lived were
| about
| _____ percent.

The Draft
_____

How did some 'rich boys' get out of serving?

| Pic 440 (bot.): Why did these Irish lynch black
| Americans in New York?
|
|
|

_____

New York draft riots

Chart 440: Was there ever a time when the South had as many fighters as the North? _____

Morrill Tariff Act

Greenbacks

National Banking System

How many years had it been since Jackson killed the 'monster bank' to when Congress authorized the National Banking System?	How many years would it be before this would be replaced by the Federal Reserve system in 1913?

Runaway inflation

Pic 441: Would you feel comfortable if you went to a friend's house and they had these potholders in the kitchen- or would you be cool with that if they told you they were made as a fundraiser?

Homestead Act

'Government girls'

U.S. Sanitary Commission

Clara Barton

Did you miss anyone? Go back and find out the role and significance of these people in this heady era. You may use the index to find their names, or flip through the chapter:

Dorothea Dix

Elizabeth Blackwell

Sally Tompkins

Charles Francis Adams

Napoleon III

Now these are such sad times / that we're all living in / for killing your brother / is the mightiest sin.   -Waylon Jennings

Quote 445: Lincoln's paramount objective in fighting the Civil War was to end slavery: *T   F*

Manassas Junction

Note the kind of parade heading out to Bull Run: | Summarize what happened at Bull Run:

Pic 446 & Quote 445 (bot.): What kind of condition were the Federal soldiers in 1) as they were leaving Washington, and 2) after the Battle of Bull Run:

   Before: *After:*

George McClellan

Army of the Potomac

Note some of McClellan's virtues: *Note some of his defects:*

Peninsula Campaign

Jeb Stuart

Map 447: Before moving toward Richmond, McClellan took this Virginia city: _____

This major battle was won by the Confederates on early July, 1862 _____

Quote 448 (left): Lincoln's reply to McClellan's request after the Battle of the Seven Days can be described as: | Q: This Confederate soldier described the scene on the battlefield as:

   a. Good humored   b. Agitated | *a. Glorious   B. Disgusting*

What did the term 'total war' mean to Union strategy? | Map 448: During 1862, this Union general marched south to Vicksburg:

Monitor

Merrimack

Pic 449: What was so special about this particular battle that it changed the nature of naval warfare?

Blockade

Second Bull Run

John Pope

Antietam

Emancipation Proclamation

Pic 452: Describe the important consequences of Antietam:

Did Abraham Lincoln really free any slaves? If you were a lawyer arguing each side, what would your main points be?

Lincoln freed all the slaves	*Lincoln freed some slaves*	*Lincoln freed no slaves at all*

Thirteenth Amendment

Map 453: How did Lincoln's policy change regarding the state buying the slaves from their owners?

| Why did the 'Democratic rhymester'
| think Lincoln didn't deserve the name
| 'Honest Abe'?

Contending Voices 454 - Summarize the views of the following:

Cincinnati Enquirer	Lincoln

'Abolition war' _____

Pic 455: The Massachusetts 54ᵗʰ, the subject of the movie *Glory,* saw action at this battle:

_____

Robert G. Shaw _____

No black soldiers ever fought for the Confederacy: *a. True*   *b. False*

Quote 454: Lincoln thought highly of black soldiers' fighting ability: *a. True*   *b. False*

Ambrose Burnside _____

Fredericksburg _____

Chancellorsville _____

Joseph Hooker _____

George C. Meade _____

George Pickett _____

Pickett's Charge _____

Gettysburg Address _____

Map 457: Gettysburg is   *N   S   W   E*   of Washington D.C.

During Pickett's Charge, Confederate forces clashed against these Union positions:

_____

Pg. 459: Examining the Evidence. What about American history does this item illuminate?

Pic 448: Which of these guys is on the $50 bill? _____

Map 458: Grant's strategy in Tennessee is viewed as   *a. Successful*   *b. A failure*

Forts Henry and Donelson _____

Shiloh _____

David G. Farragut _____

Vicksburg _____

Quote 460: What other part of the country had thoughts of secession and independence?

_____

Chattanooga _____

William T. Sherman _____

What were the following slang used for?

    Sherman's Blue Bellies   *Sherman's Sentinels*   *Sherman's Hairpins*

_____

Sherman's March to the Sea _____

Map 461: After Atlanta, when Sherman actually made it to the sea, where was he? _____

Quote 460 (right): Before you make fun of this letter's grammar and spelling, do you think this Rebel soldier, probably 18-years-old and not graduated from school, would have been happy to know that as he lay dying on the battlefield, his last letter would appear in the most used history textbook in the country 150 years later? Argue whether you think he would have been happy to know that or not:

_____

C.C. on the C. of the W. _____

Copperheads _____

Clement Vallandigham _____

The Man Without a Country _____

Union Party _____

Salmon Chase _____

Sherman's march is best described as: *a. Effective*   *b. Brutal*   *c. Both*

Pic 462 (top): Summarize what women were doing during the war according to this blurb:

| Pic 463 (bot.): In this cartoon, McClellan is portrayed as:
|
| *a. One-sided   b. A voice of reason*
|

Wilderness Campaign

Battle of Cold Harbor

Map 463: So... how'd the Democrats do in this election? _____

Map 464: Lee surrendered at Richmond after Grant took the city: *a. True   b. False*

Appomattox Courthouse

This was one term of surrender considered generous:

| Lee admonished his soldiers not to cheer in the faces of the Confederates for this reason:
|
|
|

Pic 465: What happened to the Confederate capital at the end of the war?

Ford's Theater

John Wilkes Booth

Andrew Johnson

Pic 467: How can you tell this is an event of national mourning?

Thinking Globally 468: What is 'nationalism' according to this article?

Varying Viewpoints 470: What did the following have to say about the consequences of this war?

Eric Foner   James McPherson   D.G. Faust   Thomas Cochran

If we don't fight about race, then it's about gender, class, orientation, religion, sports, politics or... wait, is there anything we don't fight about?

Quote 473: Lincoln's message at his second inaugural address was spoken in a tone of:

      a. Vengeance   *b. Reconciliation*   *c. Hostility*

Were the Confederate leaders rounded up and put on trial? What happened to them?	What do the authors mean when they write: "Not only an age had perished, but a civilization had collapsed... gone with the wind"?

Describe the condition of the Old South after the war:

"Your Government"

Exodusters

Pic 474: Describe how Charleston looked at the end of the war:	Pic 475: About how many children are attending this schoolhouse?

Pg. 476: Examining the Evidence. What about American history does this item illuminate?

Freedman's Bureau

Pic 478: Why did Andrew Johnson face impeachment as is illustrated here? _____

"10 Percent" Plan

Wade-Davis Bill

Pocket veto

Chart 479: How did legal notions about Reconstruction evolve over the following years:

1864-1865	1865-1866	1866-1867	1867-1877

Why were some of the Radicals secretly please when Lincoln was assassinated? | Summarize Johnson's stance on how to treat the defeated South:

Black Codes

Quote 480: According to this Georgian, whites and blacks had

a. good   b. bad

relations following the conclusion of the conclusion of the Civil War.

| Pic 480: Was sharecropping more like slavery or more like getting a job at a farm? Explain your opinion.

Pacific Railroad Act

Civil Rights Bill

Contending Voices 481 - Summarize the views of the following:

Thaddeus Stevens   *James Lawrence Orr*

With whom do you agree more?

Fourteenth Amendment

Reconstruction Act

Pic 483: What did T. Stevens mean when he said Southern institutions must be 'revolutionized?'

Military Reconstruction

Map 484: Note the former Confederate states in each military district, Hunger Games-style:

District 1   District 2   District 3   District 4   District 5

Fifteenth Amendment

Ex Parte Milligan

"Bluebellies"

"Redeemers"

Woman's Loyal League

Quote 485: Why were women seeking social equality and voting rights, like Susan B. Anthony, disappointed with Reconstruction era suffrage reform?

Union League

Scalawags

Carpetbaggers

Pic 486: How did this event constitute a political and social 'revolution' in the South?

Pic 487: Was Congressman John Lynch successful in integrating public accommodations?

Ku Klux Klan

Pic 488: The goals of the Ku Klux Klan were: | Southern whites tended to support them for
                                                      | these reasons:
                                                      |
                                                      |
                                                      |
                                                      |

Force Acts

Tenure of Office Act

Pic 489: What was this ticket for and why was it in such high demand?

_____

Seward's Folly

Map 490: Alaska is   *bigger*   *the same size*   *smaller*   than Texas.

While today we know Alaska was a great deal because of all the resources it has there, why did Congress authorize Seward's purchase back then?

_____

Quote 491: What was the state of the freed slave according to Fredrick Douglass?

_____

_____

Pic 491: Thomas Nast (better known as the guy who first drew Santa Claus in his modern clothes and with his portly physique) also drew this, which said that ex-slaves during Reconstruction:

a. Were fine and it was a great day for freedom   *b. Things were not all that great despite freedom*

Was Reconstruction successful or a failure? If you were a lawyer arguing both sides, what arguments would you trot out in support of your position?

        Reconstruction was a success   *Reconstruction was a failure*

Varying Viewpoints 492: What did the following historians have to say about Reconstruction?

William Dunning   *Howard Beale*   *W.E.B. Dubois*

Kenneth Stampp   *Benedict & Litwack*   *Eric Foner*   *Steven Hahn*

Pg. 496   **22 – THE INDUSTRIAL ERA DAWNS**   **Baron** _____

"Hey what's up? We're the .00000001 percent!"

Quote 496: Henry George would most likely favor:

    a. Laissez-faire economics   *b. A degree of government socialism*   *c. Libertarianism*

What does the tongue-in-cheek phrase, "The iron colt becomes the iron horse" mean in this case?

_____

Cleveland came under criticism for his "giveaway" of 1887, what did he "give away" and is the term a fair assessment?

_____

Chart 497: After the U.S., which country in the Americas had the most railways in 1889?	List the top 6 countries in Europe by amount of railway in 1889:
_____	1) 2)
Where would India be classified on this table?	3) 4)
	5) 6)

Map 498: No one likes the concept of eminent domain, whereby the government can seize the private property of a citizen by force for a supposed national good (though in fairness they pay you the market price or more), but looking at the map, do you think the railroad (or later the highway system) could have been constructed *without* eminent domain being invoked?

_____

In the poem on pg. 499, what is a 'Paddy'?	What are the 'Paddies' doing?

Pic 499: Environmentally speaking, where do you think the toughest place to build railroads would be?

_____

Pic 500: In what year did the 'Great Event' occur on the Union Pacific RR? _____

Quote 500: James B. Weaver was   *a. A supporter of the rail companies*   *b. A populist*

Pic 501: For what purpose did this ceremony in Utah occur in 1869?

_____

How was 'time itself' bent to the needs of the railway system?

_____

Time zones

Jay Gould

Pic 502: What is the meaning of 'robber baron' in the context | Are there any 'robber barons'
Of this image of Jay Gould? | today? Do you have an example?
|
|

_____

What happened in the *Wabash, St. Louis & Pacific Railroad Company v. Illinois* case?

_____

Interstate Commerce Act

Quote 504: What is Ralph Waldo Emerson (Seriously? This guy's *still* around?) saying happens to German and Irish Americans who go to work on the railroad?

_____

You know what a millionaire is, but when was it first employed as a term to describe people?

_____

Chicago became a major 'break-of-bulk' node (a place where forms of transportation switch for those of you who didn't take AP Human Geography and if you didn't then shame on you!). What about Chicago's location made it a break-of-bulk city- and what forms of transport were products switching between?

_____

Captain of Industry

Note some of the new inventions that appeared at this time, often in conjunction with industrialization:

_____

Pic 504: Who was the 'Wizard of Menlo Park' and what kinds of things did he invent?

_____

Andrew Carnegie

John D. Rockefeller

J.P. Morgan

Vertical integration

Horizontal integration

Trust

Standard Oil

Interlocking directorates

Pic 505: Does this image about the influence over government and other businesses by Standard Oil also apply to J.P. Morgan's banking empire? Why or why not?

Heavy industry

Capital goods

Consumer goods

Bessemer process

Why is Andrew Carnegie's life considered a 'rags-to-riches' story?

| Quote 506: Do you agree with Carnegie on this?
| (Or are you going to be buried in a solid gold coffin?)

Pic 506: While Carnegie and Rockefeller were producing physical goods, what was Morgan producing that is considered 'finance capitalism?'

| Pic 507: The cartoonist believes people
| like Rockefeller:
|
| *a. Respect politicians*   *b. Uh, no*
|

What circumstances brought Carnegie and Morgan 'into collusion', and what resulted?

The invention that gave the oil industry a 'new lease on life' at the turn of the 20th century was:

Gospel of wealth

Social darwinists

Which social darwinist was American?   *a. Herbert Spencer*   *b. William Graham Sumner*

Why did social darwinists take to the laissez-faire economics theory of David Ricardo so readily?

_____

'Survival of the fittest'

Pic 508: The image of the big capitalist fat-cat lazily sitting atop the mass of working people who support them, like this cartoonist is describing as a social commentary about Vanderbilt and the others, is a classic image.

What is the cartoonist's opinion of their amazing | Do you <u>agree</u>? Or do the wealthy people of the
wealth likely to be? | the world work hard to get that way as well
                                                                            | (i.e.: Is it more complicated than that)?
                                                                            |
                                                                            |

Plutocracy

Sherman Anti-Trust Act

Contending Voices 510 - Summarize the views of the following:

    Populist platform   *Social darwinists*

                                     |
                                     |
                                     |

With whom do you agree more?

_____

Pic 510: How are these images an example of | Do you think the family on the left should be
'gross inequality'? | obligated to give money to families like the one
                                                                              | on the right?
                                                                              |
                                                                              |

Quote 511: Grady was sad because the Confederate veteran: *a. Died in an accident*   *b. Died poor*

_____

'Hillbillies'

Pic 511: Who is doing a lot of the mill work? | Chart 512: As the South made more 'spindles'
                                              | England also grew in its industry:
                                              |
                                              | a. True   b. False
                                              |

Chart 512 (bot.): By 1903, the U.S.   a. Dominated   b. Fell behind   in the world cotton industry.

Pic 514 (top): Are these women the 'new | Quote 513: Polish workers who got this work
women' of Charles Dana Gibson's artistic ideal? | schedule might have understood your schedule
                                              | (If you're in school and not at home b/c CoVid).
                                              | Rewrite the ditty replacing their terms for your
_____ | terms, like 'alarm' instead of 'whistle':
                                              |
Map 513: Name three states where 25% of the |
Was working in manufacturing: |
                                              |
_____ _____ _____ |
                                              |
What industries and natural resources were |
located in Ohio? |
                                              |
_____ |
                                              |
Which industries and natural resources were |
located in your state? (if you live in Ohio, move |
and then finish this assignment). (we're waiting) | Do you think all these bells and whistles got
                                              | us used to school bells and informed our ideas
                                              | about how schools should be run?
                                              |
                                              |

Pic 514 (bot.): Do you like the idea of the 'Gibson Girl', | Pic 514/515: Whose life would you
who is assertive and interested in activities like sports | rather have- Gibson Girl or Breaker Boy?
and being in fashion? |
                                              |

Philanthropy

'Scabs'

"Lockout"

What did Jay Gould boast he could do to keep workers in line?

Labor union

Pg. 516: Examining the Evidence. What about American history does this item illuminate?

"Black list" _____

Company town _____

Pic 517: What evidence is there in this Koehler painting that a strike is happening?

_____

National Labor Union _____

Knights of Labor _____

Why does the little song on pg. 517 have the term 'eight hours' in it?

_____

Haymarket Square _____

AFL _____

Mother Jones _____

Samuel Gompers _____

Pic 521: Do you agree or disagree with Gompers that workers should have the right to strike if the firm they work for doesn't give in to their demands in a collective bargaining scenario?

| Could the students at *your* school strike? They would have to agree not to do the work until their demands were met, like better cafeteria food or whatever. It would make the news. What other issue could they strike about?

Varying Viewpoints 522: What did the following historians have to say about industrialization?

Matthew Josephson   *Gutman & Montgomery*   *Alexis de Tocqueville*

Stephan Thernstrom   *James Henretta*   *Michael Katz*

Disagreement? In American history? Nah, can't be true.

Quote 524: Did Henry Adams believe in the 'Theory of Progress?'	Do you? Should each president be better than the last?

Adams was bringing up perhaps the most nerve-wracking idea of the times, *Degeneration Theory.* The theory said it isn't progress that happens in civilized societies, it's anti-progress. As time moves forward within a civilization that exists in an advanced state, as ours has since at least the Industrial Age, the regular processes that affect people in their natural state apply less and less. Natural selection no longer applies, so the weak survive as well as the strong, reproduce, and with votes, impose upon the strong and vital. We are now living artificially, the theory says, in the society of comfort and ease which we have constructed around ourselves. And within that bubble, indeed there was no 'Washington' around during the Reconstruction era, instead, 'Grants' were. There was no Washington to take the lead, because there literally was *no* Washington, his own descendants being less than he. And in our day? Degeneration Theory predicts we weaken morally, mentally and physically as time goes by, instead of strengthen. If you don't believe it, Google: "Thomas Jefferson's letters" and read one. Or imagine why we *could* and *did* go to the Moon 50 years ago but not today. So what did *waving the bloody shirt* mean in this context, and what did it have to do with the growing recognition of 'mob mentality?'

Remember the "Era of Good Feelings?" What did the "Era of Good Stealings" mean for the country?

Tweed ring

Pic 525: Boss Tweed was in charge of this public institution, but unofficially: _____

Credit Mobilier scandal

"Turn the Rascals Out"

Panic of 1873

Pic 526: This image, reminiscent of an *ouroborus*, an old symbol of a dragon that eats its own tail, shows who? And why are they consuming each other?	Quote 528: What does Wells think about the economic crisis of '73?

Gilded Age

Patronage

James G. Blaine

Pic 529: Why would one guess that Union soldier-veterans would vote Republican in '76?

Rutherford B. Hayes

Compromise of 1877

Map 530: Which candidate did the South vote for in the majority? _____

Chart 530: Which body actually cast the deciding vote in the election of 1876? _____

Civil Rights Act

Sharecropping

Jim Crow Laws

Plessey v. Ferguson

Pic 531: How did Hayes encourage the possibility of segregation and Jim Crow in the South, whether he agreed with the policies or not?

Map 532: Draw both the before and after charts of a common Southern plantation:

Pic 532: What message do you think this kind of public execution was meant to send?

Chart 533: More whites than blacks were lynched (hung) before the year _____

The number of both races being 0 lynched did not occur until the year _____

Pic 533: What kinds of problems began occurring between whites and Chinese in California at this time that led to incidents like this one on the magazine cover?

Chinese Exclusion Act

U.S. vs. Wong Kim Ark

Pendleton Act

Contending Voices 535 - Summarize the views of the following:

Washington Plunkitt   Theodore Roosevelt

With whom do you agree more?

Pg. 536: What are some of the things Chinese did to become 'Makers of America'?

Mudslinging

How did mudslinging help Grover Cleveland in this election?

| Pic 539: What logic was used to argue for the
| protective tariff and would you have been
| swayed to be for or against it?

Pic 538: Aside from this novelty, note some of the humorous slogans used for things going on during this election of 1888:

Billion-Dollar Congress

Sip an espresso at a café in an Art Deco district and talk about a Monet painting while Debussy is playing in the background. You'll have "arrived."

Quote 544: If you'd like a world history flashback, recall the first pillar of Islam is the statement of faith, with says, *"There is no god but Allah, and Muhammad is his Prophet."* How is this quote similar?

_____

How many people did New York have in 1900?	What was its ranking worldwide?

Skyscraper

"Form follows function"

Note some new developments in transportation at the turn of the 20ᵗʰ century:

Pic 545: The Brooklyn Bridge, built in _____, was the largest _____ bridge in the world.

These cities doubled or tripled in size before 1900:

Chart 545: After which year did the percentage of Americans living in cities pass 80%? _____

Department store

What happened to the volume of waste generated by city-dwellers in this era?

   a. It went down due to recycling   *b. It evened out with medieval norms*   *c. It exploded*

Dumbbell tenement

Which ethnic groups were classified as 'New Immigrants?'	Pic 546: How many rooms had access to sunlight in a tenement?

If you were a lawyer arguing immigration policy, and in your appearance before Congress you brought the Graph 545 to address a subcommittee deciding on a new bill, which two decades of the graph would you argue should be mimicked during the next two decades and why?

Chart 547: Which nations did the Old Immigration come from versus the New Immigration?

Old: *New:*

_____

Pg. 548: What are some of the things Italians did to become 'Makers of America' (do NOT say "pizza")?

_____

_____

_____

Pic 551: America's cities like New York were: | Quote 551: This lady is ___ to come to the U.S.
                                                  |
a. Densely   *b. Sparsely*   populated in 1900. | *a. ambivalent*   *b. sad*   *c. ecstatic*

Pic 552: While they assimilated, note some ways that Jewish, Polish and Italian immigrants held on to their traditional cultures in this era:

Pg. 553: Examining the Evidence. What about American history does this item illuminate?

_____

_____

_____

Jane Addams _____

Hull House _____

Pic 554: What age groups gathered at Hull House for cultural events?

_____

Settlement houses _____

Florence Kelley _____

Nativism _____

Do you agree with the nativists that America, if it accepts too many | Pic 555: Did immigrants
immigrants, becomes a dumping ground instead of a melting pot? | *automatically* favor high
                                                                        | immigration levels?
                                                                        |
                                                                        |

What were some specific complaints the Nativists had about the new immigrants?	Quote 555: What was Israel Zangwill's take on the high levels of new immigration?

Pic 556: What did the people of France get the people of America for its 100th birthday celebration?

_____

Emma Lazarus

What did the nativists think about Emma Lazarus' poem inscribed on the Statue of Liberty?

Liberal protestants

What two new Christian denominations appeared at this time?

YMCA

Pic 557: There is an underrepresented group in America, and indeed in all countries, that very few people hear about, and that politicians generally don't think about. Orphans. Oliver Twist aside, if you are not one, you have little chance of being involved in their issues. As adults, or emerging adults, we have a greater degree of choice over our identities and future. Orphans are a group, singularly, who do not. What did Mr. Moody do to help them in his own way?

Charles Darwin

Darwin promoted natural selection. Summarize how this theory is different than belief in divine creation of fixed species:

Normal schools

Describe the rise in the literacy rate between 1870 and 1900 in America:

| Pic 559: What did Booker T. Washington advocate?

Tuskegee Institute

George Washington Carver

W.E.B. DuBois

NAACP

"Talented tenth"

Pic 560: Have you ever considered renouncing your citizenship? What country would you move to?

Yes / No   Country:

| Quote 560: What 'double consciousness' is DuBois describing here?

Land-grant colleges

Chart 561: As a percentage of high school graduates, more Americans graduated from college in:

     a. 1880   *b. 1920*   *c. 2000*   *d. 2011*

Name three universities that philanthropists, despite their sometimes unsavory reputations, donated money to open:

| How was Johns Hopkins
| University different than the
| others?

Note three examples highlighting how colleges and universities secularized in this era:

1)   *2)*   *3)*

William James

Pragmatism

Library of Congress

They say Andrew Carnegie came from Scotland at age 13 with $2 in his pocket. Note his amazing contribution to the poor man's education:

_____

Pic 563: What is a good example of the "penny press?" _____

William Randolph Hearst _____

Yellow journalism _____

Joseph Pulitzer _____

Edwin Godkin _____

Henry George _____

Edward Bellamy _____

Pic 564: Would Victoria Woodhall and Tennessee Chaflin have agreed with Antony Comstock on the Comstock Law? Why or why not?

Pg. 566: What are some of the things the Pragmatists did to become 'Makers of America'?

_____

_____

What affect on birthrates did moving to the growing America have? Why?

_____

Chart 565: In general, what has been the trend in Americans getting divorced?	In which decade did 50 percent of marriages begin ending in divorce?

Jane Addams _____

NAWSA _____

Carrie Chapman Catt

Map 568: In which part of the country did women have the most voting rights before the Nineteenth Amendment granted all American women suffrage?

_____

National Prohibition Party

WCTU

ASPCA

Who began the Red Cross and what is this organization?

Lew Wallace

Horatio Alger

Realism

Mark Twain

Henry James

Quote 571: What did Hemingway think of Twain's writing?	Pic 571: Twain's: real name was	Quote 572: James argued realist writing should:

Naturalism

Stephen Crane

Jack London

Regionalism

Bret Harte

How did the following influence the realist and regionalist movements in art and sound?

Thomas Eakins   *Winslow Homer*   *James Whistler*

John Singer Sargent   *Augustus Saint-Gaudens*   *Thomas Edison*

Pic 573: What is the deeper meaning behind this piece? | Pic 574: Why was Chicago called the
| "White City" at the turn of the century?
|
|
|

City Beautiful movement

Note the contributions of the following to urban planning and (re)development:

Baron Haussmann   *Daniel Burnham*   *Frederick Law Olmsted*

World's Columbia Expedition

Pic 575: What new transportation device appeared at this time? | Do you have one of these?
|
|

Wild West shows

Buffalo Bill Cody

Annie Oakley

P.T. Barnum & J.A. Bailey

Where and when did baseball start?   Where and when did boxing start?

Pic 541: Today we say the government appoints a 'czar' this or a 'czar' that, a 'drug czar' or a 'food czar' or 'health czar', but where did the use of this term come from?

_____

Thomas Reed _____

Chester Arthur _____

James A. Garfield _____

Pic 505: Why were the strikers mad during the Homestead Strike?

_____

Map 506: Who won the 1892 election?   Was this the person the South voted for?

_____   _____

Populists _____

Grandfather clause _____

Pic 507 (top): This group of populists was   In your opinion, who was right in all this?
brought to heel by which organization? |
                                               |
_____ |_____

Thomas A. Watson _____

Pic 507: After failing to get the two races to cooperate, | What happened to gold deposits in the
what was Watson's stance at the end of his life? | government treasury around 1893?
                                                             |
                                                             |
                                                             |
_____ |_____

Varying Viewpoints 509: What did the following historians have to say about populism?

Twain & Warner   _Charles A. Beard_   _John D. Hicks_   _R. Hofstadter_   _C. Vann Woodward_

Lawrence Goodwyn   _Edward Ayers_   _Robert C. McMath_   _Charles Postel_   _Eric Rauchway_

Did you hear that new Handel? Its off the chain

1637	Anne Hutchinson	freedom of religion
1650	Mary Dyer	freedom of religion
1691	Jacob Leisler	cruel and unusual punishment
1692	Salem Witchcraft	hysteria
1735	John Peter Zenger	freedom of the press
1761	Writs of Assistance	search and seizure
1770	Boston Massacre	right of self-defense
1777	Penhallow v Lusanna	federal vs. state jurisdiction
1780	Major John Andre	treason and conspiracy
1798	Alien & Sedition Acts	freedom of the press
1803	Marbury v. Madison	judicial review
1807	Aaron Burr	treason
1824	Gibbons v. Ogden	interstate commerce
1830	Knapp & Knapp	accessories, legal definition
1831	Cherokee Nation v. GA	suing a state
1839	Amistad	abolitionism
1842	Alexander Holmes	self-defense
1843	Mackenzie Court-Martial	mutiny
1850	Dr. John Webster	reasonable doubt
1856	Dred Scott	abolitionism
1858	Duff Armstrong	reasonable doubt
1859	Daniel Sickles	insanity
1859	Virginia v. John Brown	abolitionism
1864	Packard v. Packard	institutionalization
1865	Samuel Mudd	hysteria
1865	Henry Wirz	war crimes
1866	Ex Parte Mulligan	
1868	Andrew Johnson	impeachment
1868	Hester Vaughan	jury of peers
1868	Ex Parte McCardle	reconstruction
1869	Texas v. White	
1873	Boss Tweed	corruption
1873	Susan B. Anthony	gender equality
1875	USA v. Cruikshank	racial equality
1877	Martinez v. Del Valle	cross-examination
1878	Whistler v. Ruskin	
1879	Reynolds v. USA	freedom of religion & polygamy
1881	Charles Guiteau	insanity
1881	Wyatt Earp	
1886	Yick Wo v. Hopkins	racial discrimination
1886	Haymarket Riot	industry versus labor
1891	New Orleans Mafia	social consequences
1893	Lizzie Borden	rule of law
1895	Eugene V. Debs	federal enforcement
1896	Plessy v. Ferguson	racial discrimination
1899	Roland Molineux	rights of defendants
1901	Leon Czolgosz	rights of anarchists

Did you hear that new Handel? Its off the chain

10th Amendment

    State's rights: *Missouri v. Holland*

                 South Dakota v. Dole

                 Texas v. White

    Nullification: *Cooper v. Aaron*

9th Amendment

    Non-enumerated rights: *Doe v. Bolton*

8th Amendment

    Excessive fines: *United States v. Bajakajian*

    Cruel and unusual punishment: *Gates v. Collier*

    Capital punishment: *Enmund v. Florida*

    Police interrogation: *Brown v. Mississippi*

7th Amendment

    Jury trial: *Colgrove v. Battin*

6th Amendment

    Impartial jury: *Glasser v. United States*

    Speedy trial: *Clinton v. Jones*

    Public trial: *Ex parte Mulligan*

    Lawyer: *Gideon v. Wainwright*

5th Amendment

    Self-Incrimination: *Miranda v. Arizona*

    Due process: *Hamdi v. Rumsfeld*

    Double jeopardy: *United States v. Felix*

4th Amendment

    Unreasonable search: *Katz v. United States*

    Unreasonable seizure: *Mapp v. Ohio*

    Reasonable suspicion: *Terry v. Ohio*

    School searches: *New Jersey v. T.L.O.*

    School drug testing: *Vernonia School District v. Acton*

    Reading email and other digital information: *Riley v. California*

    Listening to cell phone conversations: *Carpenter v. United States*

3rd Amendment

2nd Amendment

    Firearms: *D.C. v. Heller*

1st Amendment

    Speech

    Sedition: *Dennis v. United States*

    False speech: *United States v. Alvarez*

    Flag burning: *Texas v. Johnson*

    Symbolic speech: *Tinker v. Des Moines School District*

    Compelled speech: *WV Board of Education v. Barnette*

    Speech in schools: *Bethel School District v. Fraser*

    Drug speech in schools: *Morse v. Frederick*

    Obscene materials: *Roth v. United States*

    Press

    Censorship: *New York Times v. United States*

    Defamation: *New York Times v. Sullivan*

    Broadcast media: *FCC v. Pacifica Foundation*

    Religion

    School prayer: *Santa Fe School District v. Doe*

    Teaching creationism: *Kitzmiller v. Dover School District*

    Polygamy: *Davis v. Beason*

Pick any eight issues and review the court cases that have established the current understanding and interpretation of the amendment in question.

1. Divide your paper into four quadrants.
2. Include the amendment number, the name of the trial, the year, the argument in court, and the court's decision on the case.

Ritual sacrifice of animals: *Lukumi Babalu Aye v. City of Hialeah*
Corporate: *Burwell v. Hobby Lobby*
Association: *Boy Scouts of America v. Dale*

Other landmarks:
    Discrimination race
    Discrimination sex
    Discrimination orientation
    Birth control
    Abortion
    Euthanasia
    Treason
Terrorism
Capital punishment
Other sentences
Jury nullification

What gives me the right? My robe gives me the right! Actually, the President because he appointed me. And the people voted for him!

Court Case	Year & CJ	Decision	Significance of Outcome
Marbury v. Madison 1			
McCulloch v. Maryland 2			
Gibbons v. Ogden 3			
Dred Scott v. Sanford 4			
Ex Parte Mulligan 5			
Plessy v. Ferguson 6			
Weeks v. U.S. 7			
Schenk v. U.S. 8			
Gitlow v. New York 9			
Buck v. Bell 10			
Korematsu v. U.S. 11			
Brown v. Board of Ed. 12			
Mapp v. Ohio 13			
Engle v. Vitale 14			
Gideon v. Wainwright 15			
Heart of Atlanta v. U.S. 16			

Griswold v. Connecticut 17			
Miranda v. Arizona 18			
Loving v. Virginia 19			
New York Times v. U.S. 20			
Roe v. Wade 21			
Miller v. California 22			
U.S. v. Nixon 23			
U.C. Regents v. Bakke 24			
Hazelwood v. Kuhlmeier 25			
Texas v. Johnson 26			
Shaw v. Reno 27			
Clinton v. City of N.Y. 28			
Bush v. Gore 29			
Lawrence v. Texas 30			
Blaze v. Rees 31			
Arizona v. U.S. 32			
Riley v. California 33			
Burwell v. Hobby Lobby 34			

JOINT-STOCK COMPANIES Investor _____
Did you hear that new Handel? Its off the chain

You are standing at the port of Amsterdam in Holland. There is a nobleman kneeled down on the dock, crying. "What's wrong?" you ask. "My life-savings is gone," he says, "I bought a ship and paid a crew of 50 to said to the East Indies and bring back a cargo of spices, but it got caught in a storm and sank, with all hands lost. Ten other noblemen came over, and as he was telling them the story, you had an amazing idea. "Wait! What if you ten form a _company_, and each of you pay for one ship and crew. Then, the company will own the ten ships, and if a couple sink on the way, the company will still make a huge profit on the ones that make it back, then you'll split the profit equally between the ten shareholders!" Brilliant! The ten formed the Dutch East India Company, and for your great idea, you were awarded a 1% lifetime royalty on all company profits.

The journey from Holland to the East Indies is indeed full of risk. But the reward is also great. Calculate the length of the journey in kilometers:

Amsterdam → Lisbon → Cape Town → Calicut → Moluccas → Batavia
      2,000   12,000   8,000   6,400   2,600

1. Total: _____ km

| 2. "As the crow (or airplane) flies," it is 11,400 km from Amsterdam to Jakarta. How much _further_ is it by sea?

3. Draw 8 little boats on top of the waves, and two boats sunk at the bottom of the ocean:

| _____

4. Each boat brought back $30,000 in spices from the East Indies. What is the total value of the company's cargo (that actually made it back):

5. What is the cut for each investor? Divide your answer for the previous question by (#4) by 10:

6. Each investor paid $10,000 for their 1/10 ownership in the company. What is their total ROI (return on investment)? In other words, how much money did they make? Subtract 10,000 from your answer to the previous question (#5) to find out:

7. During the whole year-long voyage, these 10 investors led a life of leisure and recreation. They were not working at a job like regular people, 8 hours/day. Nice life! For most people, however, you start with a regular job. Say you turn 16. You get a job. Pick one:

   a. Publix   b. CVS   c. McDonalds   d. Delivery

   e. Other _____

8. You get hired for $10 per hour. You work a five-hour shift after school. How much do you make per day?

9. This is your _gross_ income for the day, but then you find to your dismay that the government takes out taxes. You really only make $8 per hour _net_ (after taxes). What is your actual take-home pay?

10. You work five days per week. What is your _net_ income per week?

11. There are four weeks in a month. What is your monthly _net_ income?

12. There are 12 months in a year. What is your yearly _net_ income?

13. You work this schedule for two years, from when you are 16-18. You use half your total income and save the other half. How much did you save in total?

14. On your 18th birthday, you open a free stock-trading account at TDAmeritrade online, or download the RobinHood trading app. You take all your saved money, and upload $9,600 into your account. Now, it's time to invest in some companies! Pick five companies below, and buy as many shares of each as you like, but add the shares up to as close to $9,600 as you can, without going over it.

Auto:	*Ford (F)*	*General Motors (GM)*	*Tesla (TSLA)*
Comp:	*Apple (APPL)*	*Microsoft (MSFT)*	*Intel (INTC)*
Online:	*Alphabet (GOOG)*	*Facebook (FB)*	*Twitter (TWTR)*
Video:	*Electronic Arts (EA)*	*Nintendo (NTDOY)*	*Activision (ATVI)*
Media:	*Netflix (NFLX)*	*Disney (DIS)*	*Fox (Fox)*
Rest:	*McDonalds (MCD)*	*Yum Brands (YUM)*	*Chipotle (CPB)*
Food:	*Campbells (CPB)*	*ConAgra (CAG)*	*Kraft-Heinz (KHC)*
Sweets:	*Hershey's (HSY)*	*Nestle (NSRGY)*	*Unilever (UL)*
Bev:	*Coca-Cola (KO)*	*Pepsi Co. (PEP)*	*Monster (MNST)*
Habits:	*Philip-Morris (PM)*	*Anheuser-Busch (BUD)*	*Canopy Growth (CGC)*
Retail:	*Amazon (AMZN)*	*Walmart (WMT)*	*CVS (CVS)*
Apparel:	*Nike (NKE)*	*Levi's (LEVI)*	*Under Armor (UA)*
Household:	*Colgate-Palmolive (CL)*	*Kimberly-Clark (KMB)*	*Proctor & Gamble (PG)*
Construction:	*Home Depot (HM)*	*Lowe's (LOW)*	*John Deere (DE)*
Medical:	*Pfizer (PFE)*	*Merck (MRK)*	*Bristol-Myers (BMY)*
Industrials:	*General Electric (GE)*	*Dow Chemical (DOW)*	*3M (MMM)*
Defense:	*Boeing (BA)*	*Lockheed-Martin (LMT)*	*Raytheon (RTX)*
Space:	*Northrup-Grumman (NG)*	*Virgin Galactic (SPCE)*	*Procure Space (UFO)*
Oil:	*Shell (SHLX)*	*Exxon-Mobil (XOM)*	*British Petroleum (BP)*
Metals:	*Barrick (GOLD)*	*Equinox (EQX)*	*First Majestic (AG)*
Resources:	*Altius (ATUSF)*	*Lynas (LYSCF)*	*Uranium (UEC)*
Royalties:	*Wheaton (WPM)*	*Osisko (OR)*	*Metalla (MTA)*
Financials:	*S&P 500 (SPY)*	*X-Out (XOUT)*	*Invesco Tech (QQQ)*

Since the day you entered the market, the prices have changed. They change every day. Check online (google your company and the word "stock" and tally up

Ch. 24   WHAT'S YOUR FAVORITE CATEGORY OF ANALYSIS?   _____

"None" is not a valid answer. Plus, it's already taken.

The choices are: ***Social, Political, Religion, Economic***
Arts and Culture, and Technology

_____ What are people's attitudes towards recreation and free time?

_____ What worldview and beliefs exist as a general rule in this society?

_____ What is the structure and function of the state in this society?

_____ What kinds of goods and services does this society produce?

_____ Does this society use science as a tool in research and development?

_____ What are the famous literary works this society has produced?

_____ What kinds of public works buildings and spaces does this society value?

_____ To what extent does a certain pattern of belief provide a cultural foundation?

_____ Is there a laboring class in this society that has their freedom limited?

_____ What tools does this society use to manipulate the natural environment?

_____ How are people governed in this society?

_____ Who controls the factors of wealth and resources in a given society?

_____ Does this society have conflicts with neighbors over differing beliefs?

_____ Who is in charge in this society, and how did they gain that legitimacy?

_____ How have inventions changed the way people live in this society over time?

_____ What kinds of art and music does this society produce?

_____ Is there an official or semi-official class system in this country?

_____ What factors enhance the capabilities of a given society to trade with others?

_____ What happens if there is a tech gap between this society and its neighbors?

_____ What philosophies and systems of learning inform the pattern of living here?

_____ As migration alters the population, how does that affect the governing order?

_____ Is there a dynamic that men and women follow in relation to each other?

_____ Have people moved to or from this place in search of jobs or another reason?

What makes a nation's pillars high, and its foundations strong? What makes it mighty to defy, the foes that round it throng?
Not gold but only men can make, a people great and strong; Men who for truth and honor's sake, stand fast and suffer long.
Brave men who work while others sleep, who dare while others fly, they build a nation's pillars deep, and lift them to the sky. -Emerson

Quote 579: Both Frederick Jackson Turner and Washakie agree that the story of America is:

   a. An equal distribution of land between races   *b. The conquest of an entire continent*

Note some of the wars between Indian groups happening on the Great Plains and in the Southwest:

| Pic 580: This large mammal
| probably wishes Native American
| warriors never acquired the
| horse from the Spanish:
|
|

What effect did whites pioneering out west into the new territories have on the Indians there?

_____

Reservation system

What gory events happened in the following run-ups to the Battle of the Little Bighorn:

   Sand Creek Massacre   *Fetterman Massacre*

_____

Battle of the Little Bighorn

Great Sioux Reservation

George Armstrong Custer

Pic 582: Why did the | Map 581: Note the modern day states and the years for these Indian battles:
Pawnee support the |
U.S. settlers and | Year   Event   State | Year   Event   State
military forces? |
                    |_____ Camp Grant _____ |_____ Salt River _____
                    |
                    |_____ Red River   _____ |_____ Little Bighorn _____
                    |
                    |_____ Bear Paw   _____ |_____ Wounded Knee _____

Pic 583 & 584: Note the roles of the following Indian warriors:

   Crazy Horse   *Sitting Bull*   *Geronimo*   *Red Cloud*

Buffalo Bill Cody

Ghost Dance

Battle of Wounded Knee

Dawes Severalty Act

| Quote 585: Did Sheridan have understanding as to why Native Americans fought the Americans in the Great West? | Map 585: About what percent of the American landmass is set aside for Indian reservations? |

Thinking Globally 586: What is the role of the frontier in these continent-sized countries?

| *America* | *Russia* |

Contending Voices 588 – How did each think about the dance and the massacre that followed:

| *James McLaughlin* | *Porcupine* |

Who do you agree with more?

"Fifty-Niners"

Comstock Lode

Pg. 590: What are some of the things the Plains Indians did to become 'Makers of America'?

_____

_____

_____

Mining industry

"Beef bonanza"

The Long Drive

Wild Bill Hickok

Map 592: Turn this paper sideways and label the origin and destination points for the cattle trails:

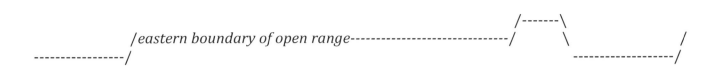

Gulf of
Mexico

/-------
/eastern boundary of open range----------------------------/   \   /
----------------/   ------------------/

Rocky Mts.

What were some hazards on the Long Drive?

Cowboy

Graph 593: About what year set the record for amount of acres homesteaded?	What kind of fraud was perpetrated doing this?

Map 594: Note the annual rainfall and the type of agricultural products in the following:

State	Rainfall	Products	State	Rainfall	Products
Western Washington			Iowa		
Northeastern Nevada			Wisconsin		
New Mexico			Your State		

Map 595: Note the percentage of the following states that are federal land:

State	Percentage federal land	State	Percentage federal land
Rhode Island		New York	
Virginia		Your State	
State with smallest %		State with biggest %	

Hey, where did you put my plow? "It's between the couch cushions."

Quote 601: In the major universities today, there is a big debate about food security. Demographers are almost certain world population will increase by 3 billion, from 7-10 billion, within our lifetimes. America is poised to go from 330 to 430 million in the same timeframe. The question of food security rests on an AP Human Geography topic, 'Just in Time' delivery. Most of our grocery stores and restaurants are stocked for a few days to a week in advance, and that's it. If the supply chain breaks, due to power outage, terrorist attack, or other black swan event, our cities would face now, in the 2020s, the same issue that Bryan spoke of in 1896. What is that issue?

Mechanization of agriculture

Pic 602: Despite inflation, the Medieval farmer would probably be _____ seeing this picture:

    a. Jealous   *b. Haughty*

| Quote 602: The author of this is expressing

    | *a. Happiness*   *b. Melancholy sadness*

Tenant farmers

The Grange

Pic 604: What were the 'fundamental premises' of these populist farmers?

Farmers' Alliances

Populists

Pic 605: What similarity did the rhetoric of Mary Elizabeth Lease have with that of Patrick Henry?

Jacob Coxey

Pic 609: Coxey's Army marched to _____ under slogans like:

| What was Eugene V. Debs role
| in the Pullman Strike

Pullman Strike

Pic 608: Here is an example of a pure racist. What is the worst thing he said, in your opinion?

'Golden McKinley'

'Silver Bryan'

Marcus Alonzo Hanna

Pic 612: The cartoonist here is making fun of industry's need for:

        a. Capital   *b. Government intervention*   *c. Both*

Pic 613: Would plowholders or bondholders be more likely to agree with the message of this Cross of Gold cartoon?

Fourth party system

Pic 615 (bot.): What did each of these campaign propaganda 'gimcracks' promise?

Gold Standard Act

Varying Viewpoints 616: Summarize with names and ideas the different perspectives on populism:

All of the following college teams have changed their names recently due to a desire to be non-offensive to Native American or other interest groups. And for good reason. Now, it's your turn. Please examine the following names, and changes, and offer your opinion:

COLLEGE	OLD NAME	NEW NAME
Arkansas State	Indians	Red Wolves
Belmont	Rebels	Bruins
Binghamton	Colonials	Bearcats
Butler	Christians	Bulldogs

COLLEGE	OLD NAME	NEW NAME
Chowan	Braves	Hawks
Colgate	Red Raiders	Raiders
Colorado State	Indians	ThunderWolves
Cumberland	Indians	Patriots
Dartmouth	Indians	Big Green
Dixie State	Rebels	Trailblazers
Eastern Michigan	Hurons	Eagles
Eastern Washington	Savages	Eagles
George Washington	Hatchetites	Colonials
Hofstra	Flying Dutchmen	Pride
Huron	Scalpers	Screaming Eagles
Indiana	Indians	Crimson Hawks
Ithaca	Cayugas	Bombers
Marquette	Warriors	Golden Eagles
Massachusetts	Redmen	Minutemen
MCLA	Mohawks	Trailblazers
Miami	Redskins	RedHawks
Minnesota State	Indians	Mavericks
Morningside	Chiefs	Mustangs
Nebraska	Plainsmen	Prairie Wolves
Northeastern State	Redmen	RiverHawks
Oklahoma City	Chiefs	Stars
Omaha	Indians	Mavericks
Quinnipiac	Braves	Bobcats
St. Bonaventure	Brown Indians	Bonnies
Seattle	Chieftains	Redhawks
Simpson	Redmen	Storm
Sioux Falls	Braves	Cougars
Sonoma State	Cossacks	Seawolves
South Florida	Brahman Bulls	Bulls
Southern Miss	Confederates	Eagles
Southern Nazarene	Redskins	Crimson Storm
Springfield	Chiefs	Pride
Susquehanna	Crusaders	River Hawks
Utah	Redskins	Utes
Wayne State	Tartars	Warriors
Wheaton	Crusaders	Thunder
Widener	Pioneers	Pride
William & Mary	Indians	Tribe

To what extent do you think names of teams, be they professional or collegiate, be subjected to scrutiny and possible removal?

Video Search: *A Science Odyssey Matters of Life and Death.*

1. Warm up: Name as many of each of the following kind of U.S. president:

     Assassinated   *Died in Office*   *Shot but Lived*

_____   _____   _____

2. After viewing the first five minutes, where would you put William McKinley? _____

3. Note three things the doctors operating on McKinley did that are medical violations today:

_____

4. Quick! Name three diseases off the top of your head and identify them as being caused by one of the following: *bacteria, virus,* or *nutrient deficiency:*

             Disease   *Cause*

1

2

3

5. What did the people of San Francisco blame the Chinese living in the city in the year 1900?	6. After the 1906 San Francisco quake struck, the reaction of medical officials was different than in the 1900 scare. How?

7. What are the symptoms of pellagra?	8. Initially, what did doctors believe = caused the disease?

9. After further research, what *actually* caused the disease?

POPULATION THROUGH TIME Demographer_____

Search: World Population Growth

1) On the graph below, sketch in the historical population in billions of people:

```
8 ------------------------------------------------------------------------

7 ------------------------------------------------------------------------

6 ------------------------------------------------------------------------

5 ------------------------------------------------------------------------

4 ------------------------------------------------------------------------

3 ------------------------------------------------------------------------

2 ------------------------------------------------------------------------

1 ------------------------------------------------------------------------

.5 ------------------------------------------------------------------------

0 ------------------------------------------------------------------------
                                                                      *
  1  1  2  3  4  500  6  7  8  9  1000  11  12  13  14  1500  16  17  18  19  2000  21
       1 = 100 A.D.                  11 = 1100 A.D.                19 = 1900 A.D.
     Rome                    Middle Ages              Exploration    Industry   Modernity
```

2) In which three regions are the world's people *clustered* in the year 1?

_____

3) What happens a) after the years 1220 in Asia and b) 1340 in Europe to lower population there?

a) _____   *and*   b) _____

4) Pause when the population hits 400m on the eve of the voyage of Columbus. Estimate how many millions of people (dots) are in the following regions:

_____ North America   _____ Europe / Russia

_____ Mexico/Central   _____ Middle East / North Africa

_____ South America   _____ Africa (South of Sahara)

_____ South Asia   _____ Southeast Asia

_____ East Asia   _____ Australia / Oceania

5) What impact did the Industrial Revolution have on Europe and the World after 1800?

_____

6) While debilitating for Europe, was the total effect of the two world wars on world population very great?

7) If demo-cracy means 'people-rule' in Greek, and geo-graphy means 'earth-study,' what does *demography* mean?

8) The most famous demographer was Thomas Malthus, because he came up with a doomsday scenario for population growth. What was his major thesis?

   a. Human population will always be fed by steady improvements in agriculture

   b. Human population will at some point grow past the capacity of agriculture to feed it

9) Below, sketch the Malthus Doomsday Graph by connecting the food dots and the population dots:

10) Why was Malthus *right* when it came to Easter Island in the 18th century?

a. They ran out of resources and food

b. They boated to Hawaii and Alaska

population •

• food

11) Why was Malthus *wrong* when it came to Great Britain in the 19th century?

a. They immigrated and advanced in tech

b. They adopted Buddhism and meditation

•
| food

• population

| 1800   1820   1840   1900   Now

URL: Census.gov/popclock

12) How many people are being added to Earth's total population of people every second:

13) In America, how many seconds for a:

Birth: *Death:*   *Migrant:*

_____ | What is the total population today? _____

14) In Environmental Science, the term *sustainability* is used to ask: "Can this go on indefinitely?" Many argue it cannot, and therefore agree with Malthus that we have a stark choice in the 21st century- to can go the way of Easter Island, or to invent ourselves out of the Malthusian Catastrophe scenario, like Great Britain did in the 19th century. How worried are *you* about how world population explosion will affect your life in the future?

Video: Carl Sagan Pale Blue Dot.

15) Do you agree or disagree with the Pale Blue Dot perspective of Carl Sagan as a way for humans to 'get along' better?

In Flanders' fields the poppies grow, between the crosses, row by row

Year	War	Deaths	Year	War	Deaths
1775	*American Revolution*	25,000	1917	*World War I*	116,516
1785	*Indian Wars*	1,000	1918	*Russian Campaigns*	752
1801	*Barbary War*	268	1941	*World War II*	405,399
1812	*War of 1812*	15,000	1950	*Korean War*	36,516
1813	*Creek War*	525	1964	*Vietnam War*	58,209
1832	*Black Hawk War*	305	1967	*USS Liberty Incident*	34
1835	*Seminole Wars*	1,625	1982	*Beirut Deployment*	266
1846	*Mexican-American War*	13,283	1983	*War in Grenada*	19
1861	*Civil War: Union*	364,511	1990	*Gulf War*	294
	Civil War: Confederacy	290,000	1992	*Somalia Deployment*	43
1875	*Sioux-Nez Perce Wars*	448	1995	*Bosnia–Kosovo Wars*	30
1898	*Spanish-American War*	2,446	2001	*Afghanistan Intervention*	2,216
1898	*Philippine-American War*	4,196	2003	*Iraq Intervention*	4,497

On the timeline below, use the data to make a bar graph of U.S. deaths in wars by year begun:

Year	0	1,000	50,000	100,000	200,000	300,000	400,000
1770							
1780							
1790							
1800							
1810							
1820							
1830							
1840							
1850							
1860							
1870							
1880							
1890							
1900							
1910							
1920							
1930							
1940							
1950							
1960							
1970							
1980							
1990							
2000							
2010							
2020							

Imagine if there was a Ferris wheel so big you could see back in time & look over the flow of ages past as it becomes our own age. Cool.

Quote 620: The Democratic platform in 1900 favored:

      a. Washington's advice on avoiding foreign entanglements   *b. interventionism*

How did American foreign policy shift suddenly at this juncture in history?

What was Josiah Strong's book called and what did it advocate?	Quote 607: Does this WaPo editorial agree or disagree with Strong? Cite evidence:

Uncle Sam

Pic 621: Noticing the 'menu' on this imperial menu, which places is Uncle Sam deciding on?

Alfred Thayer Mahan

Big Sister Policy

American Samoa

Quote 622: Secretary of State Olney's message to Britain can best be described as:	Pic 622: Note some reasons given in this cartoon for the U.S. and Britain to stay peaceful:
a. humble *b. bombastic*	

Great Rapprochement

McKinley Tariff

Liliuokalani

Pic 623: What was Queen Liliuokalani's opinion of Hawaii as an American territory?	Quote 624: Decide on an adjective to describe the tone of this Spanish newspaper:

Henry Cabot Lodge

Battleship Maine

Map 624: Place a *Yes* in the line of the U.S. annexed or otherwise gained the territory and a *no* if it was just a place where an overseas issue occurred involving the U.S. in this time:

_____ *Beijing*   _____ *Philippines*   _____ *Guam*   _____ *Samoa*

_____ *Hawaii*   _____ *Alaska*   _____ *Chile*   _____ *Venezuela*

_____ *Cuba*   _____ *Puerto Rico*   _____ *Wake Is.*   _____ *Midway Is.*

Pic 625: Could this be a false-flag? What was the role of the 'Yellow Press' in getting the U.S. to enter into the Spanish-American War?

_____

_____

Teller Amendment

Theodore Roosevelt

George Dewey

Map 626: What two events happened in Manila Bay, in chronological order?

1)   *2)*

_____

Emilio Aguinaldo

Because he was worried about Japan annexing Hawaii, what did President McKinley do?

_____

William R. Shafter

Rough Riders

Pic 627: Why did the Americans later regret they allied with Aguinaldo in the Philippines?

| Map 628: Leaving Tampa, Florida on a hot June
| day (Roosevelt and the Rough Riders stayed
| at what is now the onion-domed University of
| Tampa building), what was their destination?
|
|
|

Map 628: The three major land battles were:

What kinds of tropical problems made it so the Americans counted their blessings that this was a short war?

| Note the number of casualties in the war:

What happened to Puerto Rico after the conclusion of the Spanish-American War?

| Why did the Americans have a dilemma with the Philippines?

Pic 629: Because of the Spanish-American War and the Philippine-American War, the U.S. suddenly:

        a. Set all the peoples free   *b. Was unsure of what to do with the former Spanish lands*

Quote 630: What did President McKinley conclude about the best course of action for the Philippines?

Anti-Imperialist League

What did Kipling mean by the 'White Man's Burden' in the poem?

| Did the Anti-Imperialist League agree
| that the U.S. should 'take up the burden'

Contending Voices 630 - Summarize the views of the following:

    Albert Beveridge   *George F. Hoar*

With whom do you agree more?

Pg. 632: What are some of the things the Puerto Ricans did to become 'Makers of America'?

Foraker Act

Insular Cases

Platt Amendment

Guantanamo

| Pic 634: What visual evidence is there in this image of the idea that this was a 'Splendid Little War' like John Hay said? | Pic 635: What happened in the Philippines at this point? |

Philippine-American War

William Howard Taft

By the turn of the century: *a. Japan was rising and China was declining*   *b. The opposite*

Open Door note

Boxer Rebellion

Pic 637: What does 'Columbia's' liking of her new 'Easter Bonnet' say about American public opinion in 1900?

Pg. 638: What are some of the things the Filipinos did to become 'Makers of America'?

The two Ps

| Pic 640: Which organization carried out the unique feat of blasting out this part of the Panama Canal? | Pic 640 (bot.): The youngest president so far in American history has been: |
| | *a. Kennedy*   *b. Obama*   *c. Roosevelt* |

Hay-Paunceforte Treaty

Pic 641: How did TR manage to 'Speak Softly and Carry a Big Stick' to get Colombia and Panama to agree to the U.S. building of the Canal?

Roosevelt Corollary

What was the reason for Russia's aggressive move to take Port Arthur in Manchuria, China?	What was Japan's response?	Finally, what was TR's role in arbitration?

Thinking Globally 642 – How did the following ideas serve to rationalize and justify imperialism?

The Maxim Gun   Self-Sustaining Empires   Mission Civilisatrice   Kultur

Map 643: List the imperial holdings of the following Great Powers:

Germany   France   Great Britain   Russia

Netherlands

Italy   Belgium

Spain   Japan   United States   Portugal

Yellow Peril

Root-Takahira agreement

Varying Viewpoints 646: How did the following characterize American imperialism?

Julius Pratt   Howard Beale   Paul Kramer   Williams & LaFeber   Recent

No more fooling around- its time to make things materially better

Quote 649: To TR, what does the term 'square deal' actually mean?

_____

Progressivism

What kind of social commentary did the following authors give in their books?

    H.D Lloyd   *Thorstein Veblen*   *Jacob A. Riis*   *T. Dreiser*

_____

Pic 650: How does this picture illustrate the concept of America as a 'melting pot?'

_____

Social gospel

Muckrakers

Quote 652: Lincoln Steffens' opinion of the Tammany Hall machine was: *a. Positive*   *b. Negative*

Note the topic the following muckrakers took on in their publications and how strongly you personally feel about the issue on a 1-3 scale (1=not important, 2=interesting, 3=important to me)

Muckraker	Issue	My rating
Lincoln Steffens		
Ida Tarbell		
Thomas Lawson		
David G. Phillips		
Ray S. Baker		
John Spargo		
Harvey Wiley		

'White slavery'

'Americanize'

Thinking Globally 652 – How does this article summarize the views of Karl Marx and F. Engels?

Initiative

Referendum

Recall

Pic 653: The message the pacifists had was:

| Quote 656: How did the first wave feminists describe their objectives?

Suffragist

Red light district

Muller v. Oregon

Louis Brandeis

Lochner v. New York

WCTU

Pic 657: What happened at the Triangle Shirtwaist Company that sparked outrage?

| Pic 658: What exactly is the meaning of this ad?

'Square Deal'

Examining the Evidence 659: What do you think about the evidence provided in the Muller case?

Elkins Act

Hepburn Act

Trusts

How did people differentiate 'good' v. 'bad' trusts?

| Pic 660: What message does this cartoon have regarding TR and trusts?

| Aside from TR, who else was a great trustbuster?

The Jungle

Meat Inspection Act

Pure Food and Drug Act

Pic 661: Okay 1-10 scale, how much would you like a job inspecting meat in a slaughterhouse?

| Quote 661: Why is this statement by TR called 'prophetic'?

Note the milestones in conservation starting with the Desert Act:

| Pic 662: Where are TR and John Muir in this pic?

| _____

| Where is their selfie-stick?

Pg. 664: What are some of the things The Environmentalists did to become 'Makers of America'?

Pic 665: How did these loggers contribute to the term *skid row*?

| Pic 666 (bot.): Why did Muir say, "Damn Hetch Hetchy?"

John Muir

Gifford Pinchot

"Roosevelt Panic" of 1907

Pic 667: These people are said to be foreshadowing what exactly?

| Pic 671: Donald Trump went against his own party, compare him to TR, that is to say, what is his legacy?

Dollar diplomacy

What do the authors mean by saying Taft was a 'round peg in a square hole?'

| Pic 667: What is TR looking at here exactly?

Payne-Aldrich Bill

'New Nationalism'

Bull Moose Party

New Freedom

What was Herbert Croly basic thesis in the *Promise of American Life*?

| Pic 671: Find a symbol in this cartoon and what it means:

Do you agree with his thesis?

Map 672: While Wilson won the South, name three states that the Bull Moose won:

1)   *2)*   *3)*

"This is the war to end all wars- that will make the world safe for democracy" –Woodrow Wilson (Worst prediction of the century)

Quote 675: Wilson believes in this statement that: *a. Laissez-faire is good   b. Regulation is good*

Underwood Tariff _____

Pic 676: How does this artwork portray Wilson?

_____

Federal Reserve Act _____

'Federal Reserve Notes' _____

Federal Trade Commission Act _____

Clayton Anti-Trust Act _____

Holding companies _____

Workingmen's Compensation Act _____

Adamson Act _____

Jones Act _____

Pic 678: What are these Marines doing in this picture from Haiti?	In general, why, according to the evidence on this map, did Latin Americans accuse the U.S. of turning the Caribbean into a 'Yankee Moat?'

Mexican Revolution _____

Victoriano Huerta _____

Tampico Incident _____

Pic 680: Describe what is happening on this image:	Pic 680 (bot.): How did most Americans feel about Pancho Villa and why?

'Black Jack' John J. Pershing _____

Describe the 'chain reaction' that went down in Europe in 1914 to spark WWI:

Central Powers

Allied Powers

Chart 681: Did more Americans have blood ties to the Central Powers or the Allies?

Chart 682: Which side did the U.S. export more to in this war?

Quote 682: This message is one of _____ from the German-American community.

    a. Support   *b. Protest*

Map 683: Was the *Lusitania* sunk inside or outside the declared warzone?

U-boats

Lusitania

Pic 683: What was U-boat short for in German?

| Image 683 (right): After reading the NOTICE!
| on this, would you have taken the *Lusitania*?
|
|

Pic 672: Is this a propaganda piece? How so?

| What did the German command want in
| exchange for not sinking merchant ships
| regarding the British blockade of Germany?
|
|
|

Charles Evans Hughes

"He Kept Us Out of War"

Map 685: Which parts of the country tended to vote against Wilson?

| Why did Germany change policy and issue the warning
| to the Allies that *all* ships were now targets?
|
|
|
|

Zimmerman Telegram

Pic 686: Why did Wilson ask Congress for the authority to issue a War Declaration instead of just do it himself?

| Quote 687: Note three words in this Wilson statement that indicate 'idealism'

Wilsonian idealism

Self-determination

Fourteen Points

Pic 687: What about this message is anti-German propaganda?

| Note some anti-German nicknames
| and other labels that circulated in this
| era:

Committee on Public Information

Pic 688: This poster is _____

a. Offering money   b. Running a guilt trip

| What message did the song *Over There* convey?

Espionage Act

Schenck v. USA

War Industries Board

'Victory gardens'

Pic 690: What kinds of jobs did women take during WWI?

| Pic 691 (top): Why are these
| steel workers in Pittsburgh
| being beaten?

| How were German-related
| things treated in the U.S.?
| Give three examples:
|
| 1)
|
| 2)
|
| 3)

Industrial Workers of the World

Wobblies

Great Migration

Pic 691 (bot.): What happened in Chicago in 1919 and why?

Contending Voices 692 - Summarize the views of the following:

    Carrie Chapman Catt   *Mrs. Barclay Hazard*

With whom do you agree more?

Nineteenth Amendment

Maternity Act

What does the term 'making Playboys into Doughboys' mean?

Table 680: List the countries in which women achieved voting rights during the following times:

Before 1918:

In 1918:

1919-1920:

1924-1946:

1947-1952:

1956-1974:

After 1974:

AEF

Map 694: Of the six major Allied victories and deadlocked battles, note them in chronological order:

1)							2)							3)

4)							5)							6)

Quote 694: How did John Dos Passos feel about going to war? | Pic 693: Does this picture 'agree' or 'disagree' with | John Dos Passos? Why?
|
|
|
|

Bolsheviks

Examining the Evidence 695: The song *Mademoiselle from Armentieres* is saying something about French girls, what is it? | Pic 696: This post is asking soldiers to do what, | exactly?
|
|
|
|

Chateau-Thierry

Pg. 696 (bot.): We are all Americans. We've led different lives. Look at this image, and wonder, "Would I trade my life for that one?"

Meuse-Argonne offensive

Pic 696: What horrors of trench war does this image depict? | Chart 697: Copy the bar graph:
|
| *Russia*
| *Germany*
| *France*
| *British*
| *Austria*
| *Italy*
| *USA*
|

Note three reasons the Germans starting coming out of the trenches saying *Kamerad* just before the Americans were in danger of running out of supplies:

1)							2)							3)

Influenza

Pic 698: What was a 'Gold Star Mother'? | Did black American soldiers fight in the war too?
                                          |
                                          |

What does the term 'Wilson steps down from Olympus' mean in the context of the end of the war?

Quote 698: H.G. Wells (who perhaps ironically wrote *War of the Worlds*) was a _____ of the League of Nations and President Wilson's idealistic vision:

a. Proponent   *b. Opponent*

League of Nations

Big Four

David Lloyd George

Georges Clemenceau

What did Clemenceau demand | Why were the Italians angry | What did China get during
for the Rhineland and Saar Valley? | about Fiume? | the negotiation?
                                    | |
                                    | |
                                    | |

Treaty of Versailles

The treaty, according to the authors, was based on   *a. vengeance*   *b. reconciliation*

Irreconcilables

Pic 700: Is this cartoon's POV pro or anti- | What was the conclusion of the 'Solemn Referendum'
ratification? | of 1920?
                                              |
                                              |

Varying Viewpoints 702: How did each historian argue on the question of Wilson's idealism?

George Kennan & Henry Kissinger   *Arthur Link & Thomas Knock*

W.A. Williams   *J.M. Cooper*   *Erez Manela*

They're all around us.   *(If you ain't one now, you will be soon)*

From Ancient Athens to Andersonville Prison Camp in the Civil War, to WWI (3 million deaths) and WWII, typhus epidemics have broken out many times in prisons when conditions get unsanitary. That's only one of a number of infectious diseases people have had to contend with:

DISEASE	TYPE	VECTOR	DEATHS/YEAR
African Sleeping Sickness	Parasite	tsetse fly	34,000
AIDS (HIV)	Virus*	body fluids	1,200,000
Anthrax	Bacteria	airborne	a few
Bubonic Plague*	Bacteria	flea bite	200
Chickenpox*	Virus	airborne	7,000
Cholera*	Bacteria	unsanitary	130,000
Coronavirus (Covid-19)	Virus	airborne	1,730,000 (2020)
Common Cold (200 types)	Virus	airborne	a few
Dengue Fever	Virus	mosquito	20,000
Diphtheria	Bacteria	airborne	5,000
Dysentery	Bacteria	unsanitary	80,000
Ebola	Virus	body fluids	11,000
Enterovirus (Polio+64)	Virus	mucus	a few
Gonorrhea	Bacteria	std	4,000
Hepatitis A, B, C	Virus	blood	380,000
Herpes	Virus	body fluids	a few
HPV	Virus	body fluids	266,000
Influenza (Flu)	Virus	airborne	500,000
Legionnaires	Bacteria	airborne	a few
Leprosy*	Bacteria	airborne	a few
Lyme	Bacteria	tick bite	4,000
Malaria	Parasite	mosquito	1,200,000
Measles	Virus	airborne	110,000
Meningitis	Bacteria	body fluids	303,000
Norovirus (Stomach Flu)	Virus	foodborne	210,000
Pertussis	Bacteria	airborne	61,000
Pneumonia	Virus	airborne	4,000,000
Rabies	Virus	dog bite	60,000
Salmonella	Bacteria	foodborne	a few
Schistosomiasis	Parasite	unsanitary	200,000
Scabies	Parasite	crowdedness	a few
Sepsis	Bacteria	reaction	3,000,000
Smallpox*	Virus	airborne	none since 1978
Streptococcal pharyngitis	Bacteria	airborne	a few
Syphilis	Bacteria	body fluids	120,000
Tetanus	Bacteria	blood	60,000
Tuberculosis	Bacteria	airborne	1,500,000
Typhoid Fever	Bacteria	foodborne	181,000
Typhus*	Bacteria	lice bite	none since 1947
West Nile Fever	Bacteria	mosquito	280
Yellow Fever	Virus	mosquito	30,000
Zika	Virus	mosquito	none
Cancer	*Mutation*	*varies*	*10,000,000*

Directions: On your own separate sheet, categorize these into viral, bacteriological and parasitical sources, careful to _rank them_ by how many people die of each in an average year.

* Guess what the asterisk means and and write it on the page somewhere under your categories.

<u>Movies to Watch</u>

On Her Majesty's *Secret Service (Bond)* *Andromeda Strain* *The Omega Man* *The Stand* *12 Monkeys* *Outbreak* *Contagion*

Will the war to end all wars really end war?

Of Wilson's *Fourteen Points,* which was supposed to be used as a guide to peace at the Paris Peace Conference, what do you see as the rationale- the benefit Wilson saw- in the point?

1. Open covenants of peace with no secret dealings or treaties between diplomats.	2. Absolute freedom of navigation upon the seas, outside territorial waters.
3. The removal, as far as possible, of all economic barriers to international trade.	4. The reduction of national armaments to the lowest point consistent with domestic safety.
5. Free, open-minded, and impartial adjustment of all colonial claims.	6. Evacuation of all Russian territory and a welcoming of Russia under institutions of her choosing.
7. Evacuation of Belgian territory, with no attempt to limit the sovereignty of this small country.	8. All French territory should be freed, with the provinces of Alsace and Lorraine returned to France.
9. A readjustment of the frontiers of Italy-Austria should be effected along lines of nationality.	10. The nationalities of Austria-Hungary should be given the opportunity for self-determination.
11. Romania and Serbia should have their territories restored with access to the sea.	12. The Turkish and subject portions of the Ottoman Empire should have self-determination.
13. Poland should be recreated with access to the sea, and guaranteed by international covenant.	14. A League of Nations must be formed for mutual guarantee of territory for states great & small.

Hey, psst? What's the secret code to get into the Great Gatsby party?

| Quote 705: What does America need now, according to Hoover? | What are some things Americans did to begin a decade of 'homegrown prosperity?' |

Scientific management _____

Fordism _____

Charles Lindburgh _____

| Pic 707: A gas station is on every corner. They used to pump the gas for you. do they do that anymore? | Pic 708: Why did Charles Lindbergh lose some his fame? |

| Pic 708: Do you believe these people listening to the radio have the same addiction as people nowadays do to Netflix? | Quote 707: What is changing America more than any other thing, according to this observer? |

| Examining the Evidence 709: What did Al Jolson do to become famous? | Pic 711: What were Margaret Sanger's goals, and did she reach them? |

Bolshevik Revolution _____

Immigration Act of 1924 _____

| What were the specific overall goals of the 1924 Immigration Act? | What was the reaction in Japan to the termination of immigration from there? |

American plan _____

What alternative visions to the Immigration Act did Horace Kallen and Randolph Bourne propose?

Kallen: Bourne:

Today 1,000,000 people per year are allowed to immigrate legally to the USA. Another million enter illegally each year, but taking legal immigrants only, the total amounts to 2,740 per day. How many of the following would it take to fill the 1924 Immigration Act's quota of 150,000 *total* immigrants per year at the present rate?

Days: Weeks: Months:

Cultural pluralism

Graph 715: What was the national origins quota system and how long did it last?

Eighteenth Amendment

Volstead Act

Pic 716: What are these guys doing?	Do you agree with the authors that it was naïve to believe America could successfully outlaw alcohol?

Quote 717: How did Henry Ford feel about the prohibition of alcoholic beverages?

Bible Belt

Fundamentalism

What effects did Prohibition have on the following:

Bank savings   Absenteeism at work   Death rates and liver cirrhosis

Modernism

Lost Generation

Pic 718: Where do you think the line between 'businessman' and 'racketeer' is, and did Al Capone cross it?

_____

Harlem Renaissance _____

Bureau of the Budget _____

Adkings v. Children's _____

Nine Power Treaty _____

Pic 723: The government is selling things portrayed by the artist in this city:

a. New York   b. Detroit   c. Tampa   d. Washington DC

_____

Kellogg-Briand Pact _____

Fordney-McCumber Tariff _____

What influence on public life did the following have:

Automobile   Advertising   Sports   Credit

_____

Pic 726: These guys are trying to outrun:	Pic 727: This president did not play around. He is unsung, but he held the highest office in the land. His name was:

Teapot Dome _____

Silent Cal _____

McNary-Haugen Bill _____

Chart 729: When European countries took out loans from the U.S. government, where did they wind up?

_____

Dawes Plan _____

Agricultural Marketing Act

'Hoot-Smoot'

Black Tuesday

Pic 734: This painting is in the following fashion:

a. Renaissance   *b. Socialist-realism*

| The flappers of the 1920s were _____
| than their parents of the Edwardian Age.
|
| *a. less inhibited*   *b. more serious*
|

Pg. 737: Examining the Evidence. What about American history did this illuminate?

RFC

Norris-La Guardia Act

BEF

Pic 739: People were getting ready for war by this propaganda. Sketch out the country it was directed against (find Japan online and use it):

If you have gum in school, even if you shouldn't, go ahead and blow a bubble till it pops, and say, "That was the whole chapter in miniature."

Quote 720: President Roosevelt was   *a. Optimistic   b. Pessimistic*   about the future.

Characterize Eleanor Roosevelt: | Characterize the 'good' and 'bad' guys in his Cabinet:
                                         |
                                         | *'Good'*   *'Bad'*
                                         |
                                         |
                                         |
                                         |
                                         |
                                         |

Brain Trust _____

New Deal _____

Quote 746: How did FDR block people who accused him | Pic 746: What is funny about this satire?
of socialism? |
                                                     |
_____ |

Hundred Days _____

Pic 749: FDR actually had fun being President. What is he doing here?

_____

Glass-Steagall Act _____

Chart 748: Remember this chart. The Glass-Steagall Act was one of the most efficient and well-written in American history. Libertarians say, "Hey government, get out of the way." Here, no one, not even Rand Paul, pauses. The evidence is that when it was repealed in the 1990s under Clinton, it led to the 2008 banking crisis. That and the concentration of all the media companies into a few hands is the legacy we are living with now. If you were a congressman, would you vote to bring back Glass-Steagall?

                    a. Yes, immediately   *b. No*

CCC _____

Charles Coughlin _____

Quote 753: What did Father Coughlin stop FDR from doing? _____

Pic 752 (bot.): This is a   *a. Mosaic*   *b. Mural*   *c. Watercolor*

Pic 753: What decade do you think this image was taken in, since most of the Civil Rights movement went down in the 1960s:

a. 1930s   b. 1940s   c. 1950s   d. 1960s

NRA

AAA

Dust Bowl

Map 757: Some states have 'panhandles.' Florida has one, West Virginia has one, Maryland has one, but what state's panhandle suffered most from the dust bowl?

Indian Reorganization Act

TVA

Map 759: About how many dams were constructed to fulfill the TVA mandate? _____

Social Security Act

Wagner Act

Pic 760: What should you do when the boss won't talk? _____

Fair Labor Standards Act

CIO

Pic 761: Why do you think the term 'organize' put fear into boss men in the 1930s?

Court-packing plan

Keynesianism

Chart 765: Which country had the most industrial production in 1940? _____

Varying Viewpoints 766: Note the perspectives of the following historians on the New Deal:

A. Schlesinger   *Carl Degler*   *Barton Bernstein*   *Alan Brinkley*

David Kennedy   *Kessler-Harris, Gordon & Mettler*   *William Leuchtenburg*

A Science Odyssey: Bigger, Better, Faster (~1 min. in)

Video search: *A Science Odyssey Bigger, Better, Faster, Charles Osgood*

1. How many pieces of technology do you use in an average day? List them, from the clock or phone that wakes you up in the morning to the refrigerator you get a snack from to the light that you turn off at the end of the night:

\
\
\
\

2. Why was the year 1903 such a big one in the history of technology?

\
\

3. William Randolph Hurst is famous for selling 'stories' by increasing the font size on the titles of newspapers. What big story did he endorse and cover related to flying?

\
\

4. Describe the use of the airplane in World War I:

\
\

5. Henry Ford did *not* invent the car. You would lose Jeopardy if you answered he did. So what *did* Henry Ford do that changed the world and was the great breakthrough in the Second Industrial Revolution?

\
\
\

6. How did people's lives change when the automobile was put into service in America?

Sounds like a soap opera, but we're starting a new club, called the Popular History Front, and building a Hooverville behind the school. Want in? "Okie."

Quote 751: What did FDR appeal to Americans to quarantine?

_____

London Economic Conference

Pic 771: What city is FDR being a 'good neighbor' to?

| Pic 773: Hitler is using the pomp and ceremony to get Germans ready for war. Here he is seen as:

| *a. A dictator   b. A last hope*

|

Good Neighbor Policy

Reciprocal Trade Agreements

Rome-Berlin Axis

Johnson Debt Default Act

Neutrality Acts

Abraham Lincoln Brigade

Pic 774: This cartoon is saying the USA should remain:

a. Neutral   b. Involved

| Quote 775: Why did Canute fight in Spain?

|

|

Quarantine Speech

Appeasement

Hitler-Stalin Pact

Quote 776: When FDR got this message, he knew _____ had begun.

     a. WWI   b. The Great Depression   c. WWII   d. WWIII

"Phony War"

Pic 777: The world's most stigmatized symbol, the *Hakenkreuz*, shown here dredging its way through Poland, is generally translated into English as:

     a. Hooked Cross   b. Gammadion   c. Swastika

_____

Quote 776: If the German attack on Poland began at dawn on Sept. 1, 1939 and by mid-afternoon *Luftwaffe* planes were flying over the Polish capital, why did Roosevelt get this call in the middle of the night?

Quote 777 (bot): Hitler argued this was a war to _____ of the German people.

a. Increase the wealth

b. Secure the existence

Lebensraum

Neutrality Act of 1939

Winston Churchill

Contending Voices 778 - Summarize the views of the following:

Sterling Morton   FDR

With whom do you agree more?

Pic 778: Calling it the greatest moment of his life, Hitler is seen here doing what, where?

What did the conscription law of 1940 do?

Pg. 779: Examining the Evidence. What about American neutrality does this item illuminate?

Kristallnacht

War Refugee Board

America First Committee

Pic 780: Jewish emigration from Germany was encouraged via the Haavara Transfer Agreement (1933), whereby Jews deposited money into an account in Germany where it was used to buy tools and equipment needed to build a new Jewish state in Palestine, migrated to Palestine, then got the money back from a bank in Tel-Aviv run by a Jewish company after the tools had been sold to previous settlers. Ten percent of Germany's Jews migrated under the Transfer Agreement, to the point where Tel Aviv came to be the world's foremost example of a Bauhaus city, built in a modernist architectural style brought from Europe by the new arrivals. America was reluctant to take in many Jewish refugees, even after this event, on the night of Nov. 9, 1938:

War Refugee Board

Pic 781: This Jewish refugee, who helped the U.S. develop the atomic bomb during WWII, was:	The Battle of Britain was fought *a. On land b. In the sea c. In the air*
Along with Henry Ford, Walt Disney and William Randolph Hearst, this famous aviator advocated the 'Fortress America' concept:	Pic 782: The isolationists would have _____ with the message of this propaganda poster. *a. Agreed b. Disagreed*

Robert A. Taft

Lend-Lease Bill

"Send guns, not sons"

"Arsenal of democracy"

Wilson's campaign slogan in 1916 was "He kept us out of war," while Roosevelt's in 1940 was, "Your boys are not going to be sent into any foreign wars." To what extent do you think Roosevelt assumed the U.S. would eventually be in WWII?	Map 783: Who did your state vote for in 1940?
Pic 784: Were these mothers justified in their fear? Why or why not?	Map 784: Name the places the 'neutral' U.S. sent war material:

Robin Moor

Atlantic Charter

Pic 786: What happened in 1941 to change the situation for Britain and U.S. fear that it would be defeated by Hitler?

Quote 785: Harry Truman was partial to:

a. Stalin   b. Hitler   c. neither

Describe the reasons for and situation behind the clashes involving the following:

Greer   *Kearney*   *Reuben James*

"China Incident"

Describe the 'two painful alternatives' facing Japan in late-1941:

1)   2)

If you were a lawyer arguing both sides of the case, what would your main points be?

FDR and the government knew about Pearl Harbor in advance and were negligent	*Pearl Harbor was a total surprise and no one could have known*

Pearl Harbor

Pic 787: Describe the damage done by the Japanese in detail both in physical damage and in dealing a great strategic blow to the Americans:

Today we could use a 3D printer to print out 1,000 Donald Ducks and send them into a real war? Seriously. Sweet.

You might remember *author's purpose* from English class, when you analyze a text, art, or film with an eye towards figuring out why it was produced, the context, the message, and intended effect. During the rise of the dictators in Europe and Asia, the new medium of cartoons were used to influence the way people saw world events and personalities. As we view the following selections, ask yourself the following:

Video Search: *Donald Duck Der Führer's Face*	**Video Search: *Loony Tunes The Ducktators***
What messages does this cartoon convey?	*What messages does this cartoon convey?*
For what possible purpose was this cartoon made?	*Why do you think this cartoon was made?*
Video Search: *Private SNAFU Spies*	**Video Search: *Disney Education for Death***
What messages does this cartoon convey?	*What messages does this cartoon convey?*
For what possible purpose was this cartoon made?	*Why do you think this cartoon was made?*

Hold up, people didn't have TVs till the 1950s. So how did people watch cartoons? People went to the movies once or twice a week, and the cartoons were played as a preview, or a pre-preview to the news, which was shown as well. It was a 3-4 hour burden to go see a movie! What kind of psychological effect do you think cartoons like these had on people at the time they were shown, taking into consideration that people all gathered together in a large theater to watch them?

Quote 790: Brainstorm some some things ordinary Americans would be asked to do, that you yourself would do, and give up, so that FDR's admonishment made in this quote could come to fruition:

_____

ABC-1 Agreement

What were some reasons that 'time was on America's side?'	What does 'decadent' mean in the context of 'going soft?'

Pic 791: How many were killed in Hawaii, USA, on Dec. 7, 1941? _____

Quote 791: Note some songs sung after Pearl Harbor that are here called here nationalistic and racist by the authors:

_____

Executive Order 9066

Pic 792: Selected suspension of citizen rights is something that happens in some wars, in some countries, depending on law, and what that country's leadership thinks is prudent during wartime. The latest research shows 36,000 noncitizen Japanese (enemy aliens) were interned, as well as 14,000 Germans and Italians. To this number, however, were added 71,000 Japanese-Americans (citizens) who were brought to relocation centers, in a suspension of *habeas corpus*. Was this necessary in your opinion for either of the groups? When, if ever, should regular legal processes be set-aside during wartime for the following:

"ENEMY ALIENS"	CITIZENS OF "ENEMY" DESCENT

Korematsu v. U.S.

What were the following put in charge of?

WPB   *OPA*   *NWLB*

_____

Pg. 794: What are some of the things the Japanese did to become 'Makers of America?'

Smith-Connally Anti-Strike Act

Pic 796: How did the following organize women in the war effort?

WACs   *WAVES*   *SPARs*   *WOW*

Bracero **program**

Map 797: From most to least, note the regions people migrated from and to during WWII:

1)

2)

3)

4)

5)

6)

How did the following help in the war effort?

FEPC   *CORE*   *Migration of African-Americans*

'Code talkers'

Zoot-suit riot

Detroit Riot

Pic 798: What role did the Tuskegee Airmen have in WWII?

Contending Voices 798 - Summarize the views of the following:

FDR   *African-American soldier*

With whom do you agree more?

| Pic 799 (left): What made the code talkers so successful at 'getting the message across'? | Pic 799 (right): This man believes it should be illegal to discriminate in hiring- but for what reason? |

Office of Scientific Research

| Describe the costs of WWII in comparison with past wars: | Graph 800: The 2016 debt rang up at 19 trillion dollars. If that were on this graph, the length of the bar would be approximately:

   a. Double   *b. The height of a basketball hoop* |

"Welfare-warfare state"

Note some of the conquests Japan had in the Pacific in late-1941 and 1942:

Douglas MacArthur

Bataan Death March

Corregidor

| Map 802: Bataan and Corregidor are in this country: | Pic 801: What is historic about this particular picture? |

Battle of Midway _____

Battle of the Coral Sea _____

Alcan Highway _____

Guadalcanal _____

'Leapfrogging' _____

Chester Nimitz _____

Map 802: Note the timeframes for the following battles

_____Pearl Harbor   _____Coral Sea   _____Midway

_____Guadalcanal   _____Tarawa   _____Saipan

_____Philippines Sea   _____Guam   _____Leyte Gulf

_____Iwo Jima   _____Okinawa   _____Hiroshima

'Turkey Shoot' _____

'Suicide Cliff' _____

'Wolf Pack' _____

Battle of the Atlantic _____

"The Desert Fox" _____

Bernard Montgomery _____

El Alamein _____

Stalingrad _____

"Soft underbelly" _____

Quote 803: What did Churchill say about the Germans? | Pic 804: Where are these women going?

'Unconditional surrender' _____

Monte Cassino _____

D-Day _____

Tehran Conference _____

Normandy _____

Iron Ring _____

George Patton _____

French 'underground' _____

Pic 805: Describe the relationship between Churchill and Roosevelt:

Map 807: Note the dates of the following events:

_____ _Germans repulsed from Moscow_

_____ _Battle of Stalingrad_   _____ _Battle of El Alamein_

_____ _Kasserine Pass_   _____ _Siege of Leningrad_

Pic 806: D-Day is described as 'amphibious,' why?

_____ _Rome Liberated_   _____ _D-Day_

_____ _Battle of the Bulge_   _____ _German Surrender_

Harry S. Truman _____

Thomas E. Dewey _____

Note some reasons FDR defeated Dewey in the 1944 election:

_____

'Blockbuster' _____

Pic 808: This hand-clasping photo-op between Russian and American comrades was the highpoint of American and Soviet relations. How were the American and Soviet visions of the postwar order different?

_____

Map 808: What town in Belgium was the 'Bulge' the center of?

Pg. 809: Examining the Evidence. What about American history does this document illuminate?

_____

_____

Pic 810: Why is this German woman brought by the Allies to this prison camp looking away?

_____

V-E Day _____

'The silent service' _____

'I have returned' _____

Battle of Leyte Gulf _____

Kamikaze _____

Potsdam Conference _____

Albert Einstein _____

Manhattan Project _____

Hiroshima _____

Pic 811: Where was this iconic picture taken?	Pic 812: Note the death toll of the atomic bombing of Hiroshima:
	Instantly: _____ _Later on:_ _____

Quote 813: What did atom bomb designer Robert Oppenheimer say about himself after seeing it work?	Chart 813: The best place to be a civilian in WWII was:

Pic 814 (top): The Japanese surrender was signed aboard _____

V-J Day _____

Varying Viewpoints 817: What did the following historians say about the atomic bombing of Japan?

Gar Alperovitz	_Richard Rhodes_	_Sherwin, Bernstein et al._	_RJC Butow_	_Your opinion_

Better dead than red. Till you realize most of them actually hate their government just like we do. Then you just feel sorry for everyone.

Quote 822: What do you think Churchill meant when he said this?

| Describe Truman's personality:

Yalta Conference

Pic 823: Which of the Big Three was not fated to see the end of the war? _____

What did it mean that Poland and other Eastern European countries were 'sold out' at Yalta?

'Sphere of influence'

Map 824: This is cartographic propaganda, which portrays, whether true or false, a map that 'says something' to the viewer. What does this huge red area of Eurasia with its satellite states make you *feel* like?

| Contrast Stalin's vision of a world of 'spheres of
| influences' against FDR's Wilsonian ideals:

Cold War

Bretton Woods Conf.

GATT

United Nations

Quote 825: Baruch believed atomic energy was: *a. Great   b. Dangerous   c. Potentially both*

Nuremberg Trials

Pic 826: Why did some commentators and legal critics condemn the Nuremberg Trials?

Occupation zone

Satellite state

Quote 826: What did Churchill say has descended across Europe? _____

Map 827: What happened to the following Third Reich territories?

East Prussia: *Austria:*

Berlin: *Bavaria:*

Containment doctrine

Truman Doctrine

Marshall Plan

Pic 827 (bot): Why were these people grateful upon seeing the plane shown here?

| Pic 829: This cartoonist is saying U.S. foreign
| policy is:
|
| *a. Certain to be successful   b. Uncertain*
|

Contending Voices 829 - Summarize the views of the following:

George F. Kennan   *Henry A. Wallace*

With whom do you agree more?

Map 830: Where did most Marshall Plan aid go?

| Pic 830: What is the message of this sign
| beyond what it literally says?
|
|
|

Pic 831: What statement does this cartoon make about the motivations behind Marshall Plan aid?

| What was the main goal of NATO?
|
|
|

NATO

Describe some things that happened to shorten the American occupation of Japan:

Pic 832: Why would you want more than a bikini on while visiting South Pacific paradise Bikini Island in 1954?

| Quote 832: Was Condon right to be worried about this?

Taiwan

Dean Acheson

H-bomb

NSC-68

Pg. 834: What are some of the things scientists and engineers have done to become 'Makers of America?'

Korean War

38th Parallel

Map 836: The river where Chinese troops came over into Korea to fight Americas is the:

Describe what happened to control over Korean territory in the four phases shown:

1)   2)

3)   4)

Pic 836: Why did Truman 'take heat' after firing MacArthur? _____

Loyalty Review Board

HUAC

Alger Hiss

Richard Nixon

The Rosenberg Trial

Pic 837: Who was Nixon targeting here?

| As evidence has shown the Rosenbergs did in
| fact deliver atomic secrets to the Soviets, do you
| agree that they should have been executed for
| treason?

Joseph McCarthy

If a teacher in your school was outed as a communist, what would your position be on them?

a. They should be fired   *b. They should only be fired only if they bring their opinions into the classroom*   *c. They should be free to hold their opinions without fear of losing their job*

McCarthyism

Army-McCarthy Hearings

Reinhold Niebuhr

'The American Way'

E.O. 9981

Taft-Hartley Act

Operation Dixie

Employment Act of 1946

GI Bill

Pic 840: Do you think veterans should get preferential treatment getting into colleges and jobs? Why or why not?

| Pic 841: Why was this such a
| 'surprise?'
|
|
|
|

Fair Deal

Pic 842: Why is Truman so happy in this famous picture?

| Quote 842 (right): Conservatives
| generally _____ the New Deal.
|
| *a. Liked*   *b. Didn't like*
|

The Long Boom

Chart 843: Why do you think there was such a big increase in the national defense budget after the year 2000?

| What year did the U.S. government spend the
| most on defense as a percentage of the
| entire federal budget?
|
|
|

Note some of the things that factored into the postwar prosperity era:

_____

Sunbelt _____

Benjamin Spock _____

Pic 844: Why did agribusiness gain so much over the traditional family farm during the late-20ᵗʰ century?
(Whatever you do, do *not* Youtube: *the Meatrix* to see agribusiness in action)

| Map 845: Note the trends in where
| people were moving:
|
|
|
|
|

Pg. 846: What are some of the things suburbanites have done to become 'Makers of America?'

_____

_____

_____

Suburb _____

Levittown _____

'White flight' _____

'Wealth gap' _____

Baby boom _____

About what years defined the Baby boom era? _____

Varying Viewpoints 850: Summarize how each of the following argued on blame for the Cold War:

    Orthodox appraisal   *Revisionists*   *the Kolkos*   *Gladdis & Leffler*

ANIMAL FARM **Comrade** _____

At some point, "Four legs good… two legs bad!" became, "Some animals are more equal than others."

1. What is the original name of the farm?

_____

2. Who does Old Major declare to be the enemy of all animals? | 3. Who did Marx say was the
| enemy in real life?
|
|

4. List two reasons why the animals rebelled against Farmer Jones: | 5. List a reason why peasants and workers in
| Russia started resenting the Czar:
|
    1) |
|
    2) |
|

6. Note two of the seven rules Old Major makes for the animals:

1)   *2)*

7. How does Napoleon (Lenin) take control of the farm? | 8. What does Napoleon use the TV for?
|
|

9. Who gets the milk and the apples? _____

10. Find two examples of Napoleon's propaganda:

1)   *2)*

11. How is Boxer like a real life GULAG prisoner | 12. How does Squealer describe to the animals
| how Napoleon die?
|
|
|
|

13. What happens to Napoleon at the end of the movie? | 14. What happened that was similar in
| 1989?
|
|
|

Animal Farm Characters

Jessie	dog	George Orwell / Narrator
Old Major	pig	Karl Marx – Theorist of Communism
Snowball	pig	Leon Trotsky – Soviet Commissar, CC and Politburo Member
Napoleon	pig	Josef Stalin – Dictator of the Soviet Union
Squealer	pig	Vyacheslav Molotov – Soviet Minister of Propaganda
Boxer	horse	Russian peasants (hard workers who are abused)
Mollie	mare	Russian middle class (don't support the revolution)
Benjamin	donkey	Russian elderly people (cynical about what is happening)
Moses	raven	Russian Orthodox Church leader, voice of Christians
Jessie's puppies	dogs	NKVD agents, secret police
Mr. Jones	human	Owner of Manor Farm, Czar Nikolai II
Mrs. Jones	human	Co-owner of Manor Farm, Czarina Alexandra
The Pilkingtons	humans	Owner of neighboring farm (Britain), Winston Churchill
Mr. Fredrick	human	Owner of neighboring farm (Germany), Adolf Hitler

Russia: Oprichniki
> Third Section of the Chancellery of the Czar
> Gendarmes Special Corps
> Okhrannoye otdeleniye (Okhrana)
> All-Russia Extraordinary Commission (Cheka)
> State Political Directorate (GPU)
> Joint State Political Directorate (OGPU)
> People's Commissariat for Internal Affairs (NKVD)
> Ministry for State Security (MGB)
> Committee for State Security (KGB)
> Federalnaya sluzhba bezopastnosti Rossiyskoy Federatsii Federal Security Service (FSB)

☺ **AMERICAN COINS**   **Mintmaster** _____

PENNIES		Melt Value	NICKELS		Melt Value
Indian Head	1859-1908	*$.03	Liberty (V)	1883-1912	
Lincoln Wheat	1909-1958	*Metal 1943	Buffalo	1913-1938	
Lincoln Memorial	1959-2009	*$.03 to '81	Jefferson	1942-1945	*35%, $1.5
Lincoln Shield	2010-Now		Jefferson	1938-Now	

DIMES			QUARTERS		
Barber	1892-1916	*90%, $1.5	Barber	1892-1916	*90%, $3.5
Mercury	1916-1945	*90%, $1.5	Standing Liberty	1916-1930	*90%, $3.5
Roosevelt	1946-1964	*90%, $1.5	Washington	1932-1964	*90%, $3.5
Roosevelt	1965-Now		States/Parks	1999-2021	

HALF DOLLARS			SILVER DOLLARS		
Barber	1892-1915	*90%, $7	Morgan	1878-1921	*90%, $15
Walking Liberty	1916-1947	*90%, $7	Peace	1921-1935	*90%, $15
Franklin	1948-1963	*90%, $7	Eisenhower	1971-1978	*40%, $7
Kennedy	1964	*90%, $7	Anthony/Sacagawea	1979-2016	
Kennedy	1965-1970	*40%, $3	Presidents	2006-2016	

GOLD DOLLARS					
Indian Quarter Eagle	1908-1929	*90%, $200	Indian Full Eagle	1907-1933	*90%, $800
Indian Half Eagle	1908-1929	*90%, $400	Saint-Gaudens Eagle	1907-1933	*90%, $1600

EARLY COMMEMORATIVE					
Columbian	1892	*90%, $7.00	Oregon Trail	1926	*90%, $7.00
Pilgrim	1920	*90%, $7.00	Sesquicentennial	1926	*90%, $7.00
Monroe Doctrine	1923	*90%, $7.00	Daniel Boone	1935	*90%, $7.00
Minuteman	1925	*90%, $7.00	Roanoke Colony	1937	*90%, $7.00
Stone Mountain	1925	*90%, $7.00	George Washington	1982	*90%, $7.00

MODERN COMMEMORATIVE					
Statue of Liberty	1986	*99.9%, $20.00	Library of Congress	2000	*99.9%, $20.00
Constitution	1987	*99.9%, $20.00	Viking Discovery	2000	*99.9%, $20.00
Congress	1989	*99.9%, $20.00	West Point	2002	*99.9%, $20.00
Mt. Rushmore	1991	*99.9%, $20.00	Wright Brothers	2003	*99.9%, $20.00
White House	1992	*99.9%, $20.00	Thomas Edison	2004	*99.9%, $20.00
Columbus	1992	*99.9%, $20.00	Lewis & Clark	2004	*99.9%, $20.00
Bill of Rights	1993	*99.9%, $20.00	Benjamin Franklin	2006	*99.9%, $20.00
Thomas Jefferson	1993	*99.9%, $20.00	U.S. Mint	2006	*99.9%, $20.00
Capitol Building	1994	*99.9%, $20.00	Jamestown	2007	*99.9%, $20.00
Civil War	1995	*99.9%, $20.00	Scouts	2010	*99.9%, $20.00
Smithsonian	1996	*99.9%, $20.00	Star Spangled Banner	2012	*99.9%, $20.00
Yellowstone	1999	*99.9%, $20.00	National Pastime	2014	*99.9%, $20.00
			Apollo 11	2019	*99.9%, $20.00

BULLION COINAGE					
$1 Silver Eagle	1986-Now	*99%, $20	$50 Gold Eagle	1986-Now	99%, $1,775

So... should we burn books advocating censorship?

Absolute monarchs of the past, like Louis XIV or Peter the Great, would have blushed at the degree to which modern dictators and party leaders are able to control their societies. The rulers of the past had no access to modern forms of communication (to spread propaganda) or surveillance (to monitor their subjects). Even though they are different in their goals, the fascism of the far right and the communism of the far left had some similarities in the sense that they evolved *totalitarian* forms of government that emphasized state control over more aspects of society and the life of individual citizens than is usual in democratic countries like the United States or Great Britain. Examine the choices below, and match the form of government with the item in question by drawing a line from one to the other:

Form of Government   **Concept / Goal**

1) What is the goal of society?

Communism---   ---Form a strong national community that can compete in the world-jungle

Democracy----   ---Form a classless society in which all people are equal and work together

Fascism--------   ---Allow people to vote for representatives who will guard their natural rights

2) What are the symbols of society?

Communism---   ---Hammer and sickle representing the workers and peasants, red stars

Democracy----   ---Roman eagle, fasces, swastika, Viking runes, Nordic crosses

Fascism--------   ---Statue of Liberty, American eagle, Union Jack, red, white and blue

3) Who 'loses out' under this form of government?

Communism---   ---People whose opinions are in the minority, if their rights are not protected

Democracy----   ---Ethnic and religious minority groups since they are seen as disruptive to unity

Fascism--------   ---People 'against the revolution' who favor individual rights and a free market

4) Who are the historical leaders of this type of government?

Communism---   ---Cleisthenes of Athens, John Locke, Thomas Jefferson, Franklin Roosevelt

Democracy----   ---Karl Marx, Vladimir Lenin, Josef Stalin, Mao Zedong, Fidel Castro

Fascism--------   ---Benito Mussolini, Adolf Hitler, Francisco Franco, Eugene Térre'blanche

5) Relationship of radio, TV, news and other media to the state:

Communism---   ---Limited exchange of ideas, monitored by the state, burning of decadent books

Democracy----   ---Free exchange of ideas in the press and in public life, right to criticize

Fascism--------   ---Limited exchange of ideas, monitored by the state, burning of decadent books

6) What are the classic slogans of this form of government?

Communism---   ---One People, One State, One Leader! / Blood and Soil!

Democracy----   ---Workers of the world, unite! / From each according to ability, to each according to need

Fascism--------   ---No taxation without representation! / Give me liberty, or give me death!

7) What is human nature?

Communism---   ---Everyone is due the natural rights of life, liberty and the pursuit of happiness

Democracy----   ---Races & self-interested ethnoreligious divisions exist, build nations / cultures

Fascism--------   ---All people are equal, so class, race, wealth and national divisions are irrelevant

8) What is the role of the nation in people's lives?

Communism---   ---It is a collection of individuals who vote for their own and the common good

Democracy----   ---It is the very embodiment of the collective will of the ethnic group that made it

Fascism--------   --- It has no relevance, all countries should be abolished and humanity made one

So far, what is *similar* about fascism and communism? _____

9) What are key elements that inform this type of government?

Communism---   ---Nationalism, social-darwinist outlook, meritocracy, gender roles, militarism

Democracy----   ---No private property, collectivism, shared ownership of means of production

Fascism--------   ---Free market economics, free speech and exchange of ideas, individualism

10) What is the relationship of religious and spiritual life to the government?

Communism---   ---State enforced atheism, organized religion banned as "opiate of the masses"

Democracy----   ---Freedom of religion and belief, emphasis on secular humanism in public space

Fascism--------   ---Government support of a national religion with a focus on civic pride

11) Major are the major literary works explaining this form of government?

Communism---   ---*Treatise on Government* (Locke), *Wealth of Nations* (Smith), *On Liberty* (Mill)

Democracy----   ---*Mein Kampf* (Hitler), *Myth of the 20th Century* (Rosenberg), *Lightning and Sun* (Devi)

Fascism--------   ---*Communist Manifesto* (Marx), *Capital* (Marx), *Eros and Civilization* (Marcuse)

Do you think today's 'democratic' governments are getting more or less totalitarian as time goes on? Why?

Video Search: *Should We Fight Mein Kampf?* | Do you think *Mein Kampf* should be banned? If so, what
                                             | other books should be banned?

What is the controversy surrounding *Mein Kampf* today? |

"Roger that Houston, the Affluent Society has landed."

Quote 853: Eisenhower's message here is: *a. Optimistic*   *b. Positive*   *c. A warning*   *d. All of these*

IBM is a good company to think about when considering the miniaturization of technology in this era. What kinds of new devices appeared in America which helped increase affluence?

'White collar' _____

'Blue collar' _____

'Cult of domesticity' _____

Table 854: Looking at 2016 and 1960, state whether the relative number of women working in each of the five types of work has been going up or down:

White-collar	*Clerical*	*Manual*	*Farm*	*Service*

The Feminine Mystique _____

Pic 854: This computer was the size of a room. What size is it today? _____

'Fast food'-style _____

Summarize some developments in the following fields during the 1950s:

TV	*Movies*	*Religion*	*Sports*

Rock 'n' roll _____

Pg. 855: Examining the Evidence. What about American history does this ad illuminate?

_____

_____

_____

_____

Graph 856: About _____% of homes had a TV in 1950, which went up to _____% by 1960.

Pic 857 (top): The sector of the economy that went up most dramatically during this era was

a. Agriculture   b. Industry   c. Service

As consumerism went up as an overall lifestyle, what happened to popular notions about sexuality?

| Pic 857 (bot.): What about this image
| symbolizes consumerism?
|
|
|_____
|
| Pic 858: What do the authors call Elvis
| the 'high priest' of?
|
|

How did the following books criticize consumerism as a lifestyle?

    The Lonely Crowd   The Organization Man   The Affluent Society

'I like Ike'

Checkers Speech

Pic 858 (right): As photo ops like this and the Checkers Speech testified, what kinds of things could savvy politicians do to increase their 'brand' in the mind of the public?

Map 859: Which states in general voted for Adlai Stevenson instead of the Eisenhower-Nixon ticket?

Pic 861: What kinds of segregated norms existed in the South?

| Pic 859 & Quote 860: If the soldier and
| the African-American woman could
| switch places, do you think either of
| them would do it? Why or why not?
|
|
|
|
|
|
|
|
|

Note some of the people who were activists or writers against the segregation system:

Sweatt v. Painter

What kinds of laws were struck down in the 1940s
and 1950s that led people to believe the segregation
system as a whole might be broken in the 1960s? _____

Pic 861: Why are the people in this picture taunting
this African American girl on her way to school?

| Pic 864: Why did Martin Luther King and
| his wife get arrested in this picture?
|
|
|
|

Brown v. Board of Ed. _____

Greensboro 'Sit in' _____

SNCC _____

Operation Wetback _____

Pic 865: With immigration the key issue in the 2020
presidential race, compare and contrast the Mexican
government's position on the issue now versus then:

| Pic 866: Can you imagine cars with
| bench seats comfortable enough like
| couches that you'd actually *want* to sit
| in it and watch a movie?
|
|
|
|
|
|

Policy of Boldness _____

Hungarian Uprising _____

Dien Bien Phu _____

Suez Crisis _____

OPEC _____

Sputnik _____

Kitchen Debate _____

Military-Industrial Complex _____

Abstract Expressionism _____

Abstract Expressionism

Apollo

Adjusted for inflation, the entire Apollo Program, consisting of all the research and development of products and equipment, all the training, and the six landings, cost 109 billion dollars. A mission to Mars program is estimated by NASA to cost about the same over ten years' time. The wars in the Middle East since Sept. 11th, on the other hand, have cost 1,700 billion dollars as of 2015. If America didn't have to deal with that, how many times could we have established a human presence on Mars? Do you think that would have been a better option? Why or why not?

Pic 877: This magnificent picture was called Earthrise. It was taken from the Moon, and highlighted our wonderful planet. It gave us a sense of what and where we really are. Only, it seems, when we leave our world, do we really see it. If NASA asked you to go to the Moon for a year, would you do it?

Berlin Wall

Bay of Pigs

Cuban Missile Crisis

Freedom Riders

How did the doctrine of 'Massive Retaliation' differ from the doctrine of 'Flexible Response?'

Pic 878: The Berlin Wall was built by the East German communists to:

a. Keep people out   b. Keep people in

Pic 878 (right): How long did the hated wall stand before guys like this one hammered it down in anger?

Ngo Dinh Diem

Bay of Pigs invasion

Map 879: The original name of the capital of South Vietnam was _____

Cuban Missile Crisis

What was revealed about this game of 'nuclear chicken' in 1991 with the opening of the Soviet archives?

| Ed. note: See the map on
| pg. 879? Totally bad
| placement. We will come
| back to it next chapter.

Détente

Freedom Riders

Pic 881: How do the authors describe the people who burned this bus? _____

Vote Education Project

Pic 881: How did these cops in Alabama control street protests?

| What happened at 'Ole Miss' when it was time
| for the school to be integrated by federal
| legislation?
|
|

March on Washington

Pic 882: What did Martin Luther King wish for people of all races in his 'I Have a Dream' speech?

| Quote 883: Kennedy implies in this
| statement that:
|
| a. Whites wouldn't trade their skin color
|
| b. Whites would prefer to be black
|

Nov. 22, 1963

Lyndon B. Johnson

Lee Harvey Oswald

Jack Ruby

Warren Commission

The CIA has been blamed for Kennedy's death, the international banking cartel has been blamed, the Soviets were looked at too, but the Warren Commission went with the 'lone nut who then amazingly got shot by another lone nut' conclusion. The jury is still out on this, at least informally. Maybe in your lifetime the records will be opened. In the meantime, do you think Kennedy was assassinated by a 'lone nut' or do you think it was a conspiracy of some kind?

MILITARY JINGLES

Watch the ads, and rate 1-10 its effectiveness – in your opinion

	ARMY	NAVY	AIR FORCE	MARINES
1960			*Aim High*	*Semper fi*
	Today's Army Joins You		*v1:*	*(n/a)*
1970		*Not Just a Job, an Adventure*		*A Few Good Men*
		v2:		*v1:*
1980	*Be All That You Can Be*	*Live the Adventure*	*v3:*	*v2:*
	v1:	*You are Tomorrow*		*The Few, The Proud…*
1990	*v2:*		*v4:*	*v1:*
	v3:	*Full Speed Ahead*	*Cross into the Blue*	*v2:*
2000	*An Army of One*	*v1:*		*v3:*
	v1:	*v2:*	*It's What We Do Every day*	*Battles Won.*
	v2:	*Let the Journey Begin*	*Do Something Amazing*	
	Army Strong	*Accelerate Your Life*	*Fly-Fight-Win*	*A Nation's Call*
2010		*A Global Force For Good*	*Aim High*	
			v1:	
	Warriors Wanted	*Forged By The Sea*	*v2:*	
2020				

Why do you think there was a need for new slogans around 1975?	Why do you think slogans changed after 2001?

If you were charged with coming up with a new slogan, brainstorm one for each service:

Army:

Navy:

Air Force:

Marines:

...to finish this assignment?

Technically, the first Space Race began in 1957 when the Soviets launched the Sputnik satellite, opening the Space Age, and ended in 1975 when the Americans and Soviets declared a truce. They symbolized this truce by sending an Apollo spacecraft into orbit where it docked with a Soyuz spacecraft, and the astronauts opened the hatch and shoot hands with the cosmonauts in a spirit of friendship. So who 'won' the 'Space Race'? Below, determine by the name who accomplished what, then shade Soviet accomplishments in *red* and American in *blue*. Finally, count them up!

Year	Accomplishment	Name	Shade/write
1957	first satellite	*Sputnik I*	→ ___**Red**___ ← shade/write
1957	first dog in space	Laika, on *Sputnik 2*	
1958	first scientific discovery	*Explorer I* found Van Allen Belts	
1959	first Moon flyby	*Luna I*	
1960	first return of living things	Belka and Strelka on *Sputnik 2*	
1961	first primate in space	Ham, on *Mercury 5*	
1961	first man in space	Yuri Gagarin, on *Vostok I*	
1961	first piloted spacecraft	Alan Shepherd on *Freedom 7*	
1961	first Venus flyby	*Venera I*	
1963	first woman in space	Valentina Tereshkova on *Vostok 6*	
1964	first crew in space	*Voskhod I*	
1965	first spacewalk	Alexei Leonov on *Voskhod 2*	
1965	first Mars flyby	*Mariner 4*	
1965	first orbital rendezvous	*Gemini 6* and *7*	
1966	first Moon lander	*Luna 9*	
1966	first orbital docking	*Gemini 8* and *Agena Target Vehicle*	
1966	first Moon orbiter	*Luna 10*	
1968	first ultraviolet observatory	NASA-*OAO-2*	
1969	first crew exchange	*Soyuz 4* and *5*	
1968	first men to circle Moon	*Apollo 8*	
1969	first man on the Moon	Neil Armstrong on *Apollo 11*	
1970	first rescue mission	*Apollo 13*	
1970	first Moon sample return	*Luna 16*	
1970	first Moon rover	*Lunokhod 1*	
1970	first X-ray observatory	NASA-*Uhuru*	
1970	first Venus lander	*Venera 7*	
1971	first space station	*Salyut 1*	
1971	first car driven on Moon	*Apollo 15*	
1971	first Mars orbiter	*Mariner 9*	
1972	first gamma-ray observatory	NASA-*SAS 2*	
1973	first Jupiter flyby	*Pioneer 10*	
1974	first Mercury flyby	*Mariner 10*	
1975	first USA-USSR rendezvous	*Apollo-Soyuz*	

Technically, at this point, the first Space Race ends. At this point, not only does the focus shift to cooperation instead of competition, but new space agencies appear in other countries. Presently, the following space agencies all operate satellites: Australia [ASA], China [CNSA], Europe [ESA], India [IRSO], Israel [ISA], Iran [ISA], Japan [JAXA], North Korea [NADA], South Korea [KARI], and Ukraine [NSAU.

1. Which country had the most 'first' accomplishments?   *a. USA*   *b. USSR*

2. What accomplishment do you think was the most amazing of all of them, and why?

1975	first Venus orbiter	*Venera 9*
1976	first Sun flyby	*Helios 2*
1976	first Mars lander	*Viking 1*
1979	first Saturn flyby	*Pioneer 11*
1981	first space shuttle	*Columbia*
1983	first infrared observatory	NASA-*IRAS*
1984	first free-floating spacewalk	McCandless, *STS-41*
1986	first Uranus flyby	*Voyager 2*
1986	first long-term space station	*Mir*
1986	first comet flyby	Roscosmos-*Vega 1*
1989	first Neptune flyby	*Voyager 2*
1989	first microwave telescope	NASA-*COBE*
1990	first optical observatory	*Hubble ST*
1991	first asteroid flyby	*Galileo*
1992	first Sun orbiter	*Ulysses*
1995	first Jupiter orbiter	*Galileo*
1997	first radio observatory	JAXA-*HALCA*
1997	first Mars rover	*Pathfinder*
1998	first international station	*ISS*
2000	first asteroid orbiter	ESA-*Shoemaker*
2001	first asteroid lander	ESA-*Shoemaker*
2001	first tourist in space	Mark Shuttleworth
2004	first Saturn orbiter	ESA-*Cassini*
2004	first Titan lander	ESA-*Huygens*
2006	first comet sample return	NASA-*Stardust*
2009	first exoplanet observatory	*Kepler Telescope*
2010	first asteroid sample return	JAXA-*Hayabusa*
2011	first Mercury orbiter	*Messenger*
2012	first interstellar probe	*Voyager 1*
2014	first comet lander	ESA-*Rosetta*
2015	first Ceres orbiter	*Dawn*
2015	first Pluto flyby	*New Horizons*
2015	first soft landing of rockets	SpaceX *Falcon-9*
2015	first food grown in space	NASA/JAXA on *ISS*
2018	first asteroid rover	JAXA-*Hayabusa 2*
2019	first food grown on Moon	CNSA-*Chang'e 4*

3. From 1975 until today, exploration continued. List all the planets and objects that been visited to these varying degrees:

a. *Flyby:*

_____

b. *Orbited:*

_____

c. *Landed on:*

_____

d. *Rover:*

_____

e. *Sample Return:*

_____

f. *Visited by people:*

_____

4. Below is the Electromagnetic Spectrum. The shortest wavelengths are on the left and they get bigger to the right. Put a check into the areas we can observe:

Gamma Rays	X-Rays	UV Rays	Optical-Visible	Infrared	Microwave	Radio
|	|	|	|	|	|	|
|	|	|	|	|	|	|

5. Which part of the EM spectrum gives people sunburns?

_____

6. Which part heats up food and carries cell phone signals?

_____

7. The shorter the wave, the more dangerous to people. Which is the most dangerous wave in the universe?

_____

8. Which waves are all around us, invisible, yet completely harmless

_____

9. If you were advising NASA, what would you suggest to them we should do next?

THE WORST GAME OF CHICKEN. EVER.

Don't flinch. Unless doing so would keep the world from being destroyed.

1. What kinds of school 'threats' do people worry about and practice drills for today? List some:

_____

During the Cold War, it was the threat of nuclear war that freaked people out. In fact, some of the very first school documentaries were actually training videos on what to do if you saw a mushroom cloud nearby (if possible, see a quick clip of the *Tsar Bomba*, the biggest nuke ever).

Clip 1: Duck and Cover (1951).

2. What advice does the video give to students?	3. Was this good advice in your considered opinion? Why or why not?

Clip 2: U.S. Office of Civil Defense Fallout When and How to Protect Yourself.

4. What is 'fallout' and what does the government tell you to do if some is around?	5. Do you think videos like these were made to calm people, or scare them?

On a 1-10 scale, people during the 1950s were at nuclear scare level 7. People in the 1960s during the Cuban Missile Crisis were at scare level 10, while in the 1970s during détente they were at scale level 5. In the 1980s it heated up again to scare level 7, then the Cold War ended.

6. Where would you rate *your* scare level today?

1 2 3 4 5 6 7 8 9 10

7. In the movie *Sum of All Fears*, released just after Sept. 11, 2001, an American city is nuked. What city?

a. Washington b. Baltimore c. Miami

This came closest to actually happening during the Cuban Missile Crisis in 1963. When Fidel Castro and his communist revolutionaries overthrew the Cuban government in 1957, Moscow couldn't have been happier. Khrushchev rolled out the red carpet (get it, red?) for Castro, and the two struck a deal. The Soviets were aiming (get it, aiming?) to put nukes close to America, and what better place than Cuba, only 90 miles from Key West? This would have most likely been bad for world security, but the Americans were not innocent in all this. Most Americans didn't know, but the U.S. had places nukes of its own near the Soviet border, just across the Black Sea in Turkey! In fact, from his Yalta dacha, Premier Khrushchev could point into the sea and say to his friends, "You can't see them, but they (the American nukes) are pointed right at us".

Clip 3: TED Cuban Missile Crisis.

Clip 4: CNN Cuban Missile Crisis Counterfactual.

8. How is Vasily Arkhipov an 'unsung hero'?

9. What were the (unrealized) U.S. plans for war?

FLAGS AND THEIR MEANINGS

Flyer _____

Web search: *CIA World Factbook Flags of the World*

Directions: For **each letter** of the alphabet, select **one** flag, preferably of a Latin American country or former Asian or African colony that became independent after WWII, and research:

Country	Most interesting thing about it (click 'flag' button)	☺ sketch flag ☺
a.		
b.		
c.		
d.		
e.		
f.		
g.		
h.		
i.		
j.		
k.		
l.		

m.

n.

o.

p.

q.

r.

s.

t.

u.

v.

w.

x.

y.

z.

Some say liberalism is the ideology of Western suicide. Others say it is our salvation. It can be one or the other, but it can't be both.

Quote 886: Whose windows were being shaken and who is doing the shaking in Dylan's lyric?	Note some of the things going on that changed American life in the stormy sixties:

The 'Johnson treatment'

Barack Obama famously gaffed by bestowing upon the Queen of England- 82-years-old at the time- an *iPod* during their first official meeting in 2009. Soon after, the Obamas gave British Prime Minister Gordon Brown a set of 25 DVDs containing movies he already had. Both of these were considered trash gifts bordering on insulting. By contrast, Brown got the Obamas a pen holder made from wood carved out of an anti-slave ship. How would you classify LBJ's gift to the pope?

Civil Rights Act

Affirmative Action

Do you agree with Johnson that Affirmative Action, the legal requirement that businesses above a certain size hire a certain percentage of nonwhite males and women, fulfills the ideal of 'equal opportunity'? Or do you agree with his opponents that equal opportunity should be based solely on merit and the decisions arrived at by the business owners themselves?

Great Society

Barry Goldwater

Pic 887: What emotion was Goldwater appealing to by using this shock ad? _____

Tonkin Gulf Resolution

Map 888: Where did Goldwater do well?	List some of the consequences of the following Great Society Programs:
	Poverty:
	Transportation:
	Arts:

Education:

Medicare:

Medicaid:

Immigration:

'Family unification':

'Head Start':

Desegregation:

Immigration and Nationality Act

Freedom Summer

Mississippi Freedom Democratic party

Graph 890: On a whole, did the Great Society's 'War on Poverty' make much of a dent?	Pic 891: What happened at Selma, Alabama?

Voting Rights Act

Watts Riot

Black separatism

Malcolm X

Black Panther Party

Black Power

Contending Voices 892 - Summarize the views of the following:

Martin Luther King	*Malcolm X*

With whom do you agree more?

Marcus Garvey

What similarities did the Newark and Detroit riots share?

Viet Cong

Operation Rolling Thunder

What was Johnson's strategy and did it work?	Why do the authors write, "The South Vietnamese were becoming spectators in their own war?

Six-Day War

What territories did Israel acquire in 1967 following the Six-Day War?

Antiwar demonstrations

Pic 896: The major handicap of the U.S. in the Vietnam war was a lack of: *a. Technology* *b. National will to win*	Map 897: List the states that George Wallace won:

"Hell no, we won't go!"

William Fulbright

"Doves"

Pic 893: What kinds of things did doves and other antiwar people find disturbing about the war in Viet Nam that they did not find 'wrong' about WWII or even WWI?	LBJ dropped a metaphorical bomb on America on March 31, 1968. What was it and how did it serve to protect the status quo?

Tet Offensive

Hubert H. Humphrey

Was there a political motive behind the Arab American's murder of Robert Kennedy in 1968?	Pic 896: Why was all this extra security needed at the DNC in Chicago in 1968?

'Hawk'

Spiro Agnew

George Wallace

George Wallace was the last presidential contender in the history of the United States to run against the mandatory racial integration of the country.

What was his slogan?	*What did he do at the University of Alabama*	*What was his Vietnam stance?*

Map 897: What were the final stats in the hotly contested 1968 election?

Candidate	Electoral Votes	Popular Votes	Areas of U.S. won
Richard Nixon			
Hubert Humphrey			
George Wallace			

Many of the young people growing up in the late-1960s were angry about all authority. What do the things they were upset about mean to you- as in- how do you define these for yourself?

| *Racism* | *Sexism* | *Imperialism* | *Oppression* |

If you were growing up at this time, do you think you would have been rebellious? About what?

Thinking Globally 898: How did the following people and places contribute to the atmosphere of the '60s?

Herbert Marcuse, C. Wright Mills, Frantz Fanon & Jean-Paul Sartre   *Che, Ho, Lumumba & Mao*

Chinese Cultural Revolution   *The Prague Spring*   *Paris protests*

Tlatelolco Rally   *"Post-Materialist" concerns*   *Culture of repudiation of authority*

Stonewall Rebellion _____

SDS _____

YAF _____

Vietnamization _____

Nixon Doctrine _____

Pic 901: What happened in New York at this time | Pic 902: How did Vietnam vets protest the war?
to make it a hotbed of the counterculture |
movement? |
                                               |

What did the phrase 'the greening of America' mean (hint: not environmental!):

_____

Silent Majority _____

Kent State Strategy _____

'Silent majority' _____

My Lai massacre _____

Quote 903: What kinds of things about Vietnam demoralized this U.S. Marine?

_____

Pic 905: Some consider this to be a poignant photograph while others consider it terrible. Others consider it other things. What do you consider it?

_____

Miranda warning
_____

Pic 906: What is this sign saying? | Pic 907: How was the Vietnam
| War seen in Europe?
|
|
|
|

_____

EPA
_____

Earth Day
_____

Southern Strategy
_____

Primary Elections
_____

Pic 909: Why is this dinner so unique in the history | Would you think America intervened if
of the Cold War? | you were Chilean in this era? Why?
|
|
|

Pic 910: Note some of the cases and decisions that made many (like the people who made this sign) accuse the Supreme Court of 'judicial activism' above and beyond their intended powers:

    Case   *Controversial Decision*

_____

Miranda Warning
_____

Food Stamps
_____

SSI
_____

AFDC
_____

Philadelphia Plan
_____

EPA

Pic 904: Why did Racheal Carson's book *Silent Spring* help make her 'mother of the conservation movement'? | Pic 905: Would these Europeans tend to agree with the Hawks or the Doves?

Earth Day

Clean Air Act

OSHA

CPSC

'Nanny state'

Why did Nixon take the U.S. dollar off the gold standard and what was the reaction?

Southern strategy

DMZ

George McGovern

Twenty-Third Amendment

Map 878: On a separate paper, draw a free-hand map of Viet Nam and label the events. | How did the Vietnam War wind up?

War Powers Act

Yom Kippur War

'Energy crisis'

Pic 907: If you saw this sign at a gas station next time you went to get some gas, what would your reaction be? | Pic 907 (bot.): What does the Arab oil man want from this guy?

Most American cars in the 1940s-1970s were:

a. small and fuel-efficient   *b. big and gas-guzzling*

International Energy Agency

Cadillac was always a symbol of the huge cars built by the Detroit automakers. In 1976, it came out with 'the last of the giants,' the Cadillac Fleetwood Brougham. Weighing in at over 5,200 pounds, it was 20 feet long, with "a hood long enough to serve as a pool table." The largest regular production car ever made, it was driven by an 8.2 liter, 500 cubic inch engine. In 1977, all GM, Ford and Chrysler cars, including the mighty Cadillac and the Lincoln Continental, were scaled down to compete with the foreign imports. What led U.S. automakers to start producing smaller cars at this point in history?

What is your favorite kind of car? Would you pay more in gas to get more luxury or room on the inside? Make a list of some of the things you would look for in your dream car:

Varying Viewpoints 908: What did the following historians argue about the Sixties?

Conservatives	Liberals	Van Deberg & P. Joseph
Jacquelyn Hall	Matusow & Schwarz	Charles Murray
Lawrence Meade	John Lewis Gaddis	Adam Garfinkle
Gitlin & Wells	William O'Neal	Kazin & Isserman
Sara Evans	McGirr & Perlstein	Rebecca Klatch

What do you want to do today? "Overturn the existing society dude." What do we replace it with? "I don't know, something groovy!"

Quote 914: What was President NixonO opinion in the State of the Nation address of 1975?	Quote 915: What is Nixon claiming here?
a. Optimistic *b. Pessimistic*	

Stagflation

Watergate scandal

In 2013, a scandal broke in which the Internal Revenue Service (IRS), which collects taxes and audits businesses and people it thinks are being dishonest on their tax forms, was accused of targeting Republicans and conservatives under the Obama Administration. Is there a precedent for this kind of accusation in U.S. history? State your case:

Gerald Ford

Pic 917: What is going on in this comic?	Pic 916: What was contained in the 'Smoking Gun' tape that was so incriminating?

Pg. 916: Examining the Evidence. In your opinion, should taped White House discussions be public record, or do you agree with Nixon that presidents should have some privacy?

Pic 918: Thinking Globally. What is inflation in this context?	Graph 919: Despite making an average of 50k instead of 5k as in 1960, why don't Americans 'feel' wealthier now- according to this chart?

Johnson is blamed for triggering the inflation by spending a lot of public money. What kinds of things did he spend it on?	By spending on Middle East wars and record welfare state outlays simultaneously, Bush and Obama continued Johnson's pattern:
	a. True *b. False*

Gerald Ford was bizarre as a president because he was:

a. Not the VP on the Nixon ticket   *b. Appointed by Congress*   *c. Both of these*

What did Ford do that shocked the country regarding Nixon?

| What did the Helsinki Accords, the diplomatic
| highlight of the Ford presidency, accomplish?
|
|
|
|

Pic 920: Why did Ford and Kissinger stop using the term détente?

Note the final costs of the Vietnam War after the U.S. pulled out in 1975:

Money spent: *Deaths:*   *Wounded:*

What else did America seem to have 'lost' in Vietnam aside from the physical costs?

ERA

Pic 921: Before *Roe v. Wade* (1973), what was the law regarding abortions?

| There have been over 50,000,000 abortions performed
| in America since *Roe v. Wade*. What do you think the
| law should be about it?
|
|

Pg. 922: What are some of the things the Vietnamese have done to become 'Makers of America'?

Pg. 924: What are some of the things Feminists have done to become 'Makers of America'?

Pic 926: The three reasons Phyllis Schlafly cited for being against ERA were:

1)

2)   *3)*

Note the significance of the following cases:

Milliken v. Bradley:

Bakke case:

United States v. Wheeler:

Pic 927: What is going on in this picture?

_____

New Right

Jimmy Carter

Pic 929: What did the following sides promise to do at the Camp David Accords?

    Israelis   *Palestinians*

_____

Under Carter, the fate of the Panama Canal was decided. What was it?

_____

'Oil shock'

Why is it that people on fixed incomes like the elderly, and people who put money in the bank to save it, get hurt financially when inflation is high (as it continued to be under Carter)?

_____

Iranian Revolution

Malaise speech

Quote 931: Do you think Carter's words still hold true about the America you know today? Why or why not?

_____

Graph 930: Summarize the meaning of this graph: | What do you think will happen to prices
| in the future, say, five years from now?
|
|
|

Pic 932: What was Milton Friedman's opinion of government management over the U.S. economy?

(Ask your teacher if you can get extra credit if you watch all 10 parts of *Free to Choose* on Youtube)

Contending Voices 932 - Summarize the views of the following:

        Lewis Powell   *Douglas Fraser*

With whom do you agree more?

SALT II

Iran hostage crisis

Leonid Brezhnev

How did the 1980 Olympics illustrate Cold War tension?

It's morning in America. "Wait, don't hit snooze! Noooooooooo!"

Quote 938: Which amendment of the Bill of Rights was Reagan promising to defend in this statement? (If you forgot them they are in the appendix on pg. A-14)

| The slogan of Reagan's campaign in
| 1980 was:
|
|
|

'Moral Majority'

On social issues like abortion, pornography, homosexuality, Feminism and hiring preferences for minority groups, Reagan:

a. Favored restriction   *b. Favored encouragement*

| Note jobs Reagan had before
| president:
|
|_____

Ted Kennedy

Chappaquiddick

Pic 939: Reagan cultivated an image of:

a. Youth   *b. Down-home values*   *c. both*

| Map 939: Reagans victory in 1980 was:
|
| *a. contested*   *b. a landslide*
|

Quote 940: Reagan made the following arguments to bolster the conservative case for prayer being allowed in schools again:

| Reagan was _____
| New Deal & Great Society-
| style programs:
|
| *a. for*   *b. against*
|

Margaret Thatcher

Pic 940: This was a major foreign policy success on Reagan's first day in office:

| Pic 941: Why is the right side of the White
| House connected to the U.S. Capitol building?
|
|

Prop. 13

Boll weevils

Supply-side economics

Yuppies

According to the Washington Post, the U.S. trade deficit for 2015 was over 484 billion dollars. Is this more or less than during the Reagan era?

SDI

Pic 943: Whether Reagan was bluffing or not, Star Wars totally demoralized the Soviet leadership. What is this comic trying to say about the reality of his statements?

Solidarity

Note the significance of the following:

Sanctions on USSR and Poland   *Downing of Korean airliner*

1984 Olympics in LA   *Beirut barracks attack*

Sandinistas   *'Contras'*

Granada   *1984 Election*

Perestroika

Glasnost

Map 944: The U.S. dealt weapons to _____ | The U.S. dealt weapons to _____ during the Reagan '80s:
Before the Reagan '80s: |
                                        | *a. Iraq*   *b. Iran*   *c. Somalia*
a. Iraq   *b. Iran*   *c. Somalia* |
                                        | The U.S. sold weapons to Saudi Arabia: *a. True b. False*
_____ was attacked |_____
by the Soviet Union in the 1980s.

INF Treaty

Iran-Contra Affair

Pic 945 (top): In a series of summit meetings, | Pic 946: Why is this dude's hat hilarious?
Reagan met this Soviet leader: |
                                             |
                                             |
                                             |

Quote 945: Do you find this statement funny in any way? Why?

___

Moral Majority

Identity Politics

Black Monday

George H.W. Bush (41)

Pic 950: How did Bush's campaign slogan in 1988 contrast with Reagan's hardline image?	Pic 951: Would you stand in front of the tanks like this guy to achieve a political goal? If so, what would that goal be?

The following Soviet satellite states held free and multi-party elections in 1989:

___

Mikhail Gorbachev

Boris Yeltsin

Pic 952: How was Lenin an 'idol'?	One communist country erupted into civil war when it broke up. It was:

New World Order

START II

Map 953: Note the events that took place in the following:

Poland:

East Germany:

Czechoslovakia:

Russia:

Chechnya:

Yugoslavia:

Kosovo:

Contending Voices 954 - Summarize the views of the following:

    Margaret Thatcher   *Mikhail Gorbachev*

                                     |
                                     |

With whom do you agree more?

Ethnic cleansing

Since the end of the Cold War, anticommunism is no longer much of an animating force for Americans to get behind. Do you think there are any overriding issues that everyone can stand up for today? Or do you think society is doomed to be divided in opinion and sympathy?

Nelson Mandela

Manuel Noriega

Operation Desert Storm

Map 955: Note the following places using the map:

Location of Allied central command: *Countries targeted by Iraqi Scud missiles:*

Bodies of water with Allied naval forces:

ADA

Clarence Thomas

Sexual harassment

Newt Gingrich

Pic 956: The U.S. lost 148 soldiers in the Gulf War (1990-1991), and 4,425 in the Iraq War (2003-2012). Dividing, what percentage of the deaths in the Iraq War died in the Gulf War?	Pic 957: Why did the scene in this picture not comport with Bush's promise of "Read my lips, no new taxes?"

Varying Viewpoints 954: How did the following argue regarding the origins of modern conservatism?

Daniel Bell   Alan Brinkley

The Edsalls   Ron Formisano

Kim Phillips-Fein   Rick Perlstein

Lisa McGirr   Lizabeth Cohen

Shulman & Cowie   Critchlow & Dochuk

At the end of history lies the undiscovered country. In this case, the America of the present and the future. Our America.

Quote 961: What do you think Clinton means here by 'global village'?

_____

Bill Clinton _____

Al Gore _____

DLC _____

Map 962: Although he won zero electoral votes, almost 20,000,000 voted for _____

"Don't ask, don't tell" _____

Pic 962: Bill was the only president to have been a Rhodes scholar, and Hillary was the only First Lady to have also been a U.S. senator, when she ran and won in this state:	In the 1990s, the U.S. lowered its overall violent crime rate, primarily by:

Quote 964: Which demographic was the Newt Gingrich-inspired Contract with America targeting?

_____

Contract with America _____

Oklahoma City bombing _____

Pic 960: How did McVeigh cause all this damage?	What was McVeigh's fate?

Graph 961: While historically the primary source for immigrants coming to the U.S. was Europe, these two places have surpassed Europe since 1970:

_____

Welfare Reform Bill _____

Pg. 966: What are some of the things the Latinos have done to become 'Makers of America?'

Contending Voices 968 - Summarize the views of the following:

Joe Lieberman   Marian Edelman

|
|
|
|
|
|

With whom do you agree more?

_____

Bob Dole

_____

'Soccer moms'

_____

Note how the following affected the affirmative action debate:

Prop. 209   Hopwood v. Texas

_____

Graph 969: The overall pattern reflects increasing | Quote 969: Was Steele for or against
                                                    | affirmative action in principle?
a. urbanization   b. suburbanization |
                                                    |

Explain why the following deaths agitated race relations so much in the U.S. during the 1990s?

Rodney King death   Nicole Brown Simpson death

_____

Pic 970: Clinton gave tax breaks to African American | Pic 971: These people fear NAFTA will
communities in the hope the money would be: | take away:
                                                      |
                                                      |

NAFTA

_____

WTO

_____

This was not something that helped spur the 1990s boom-time economy for better or worse:

a. Federal Reserve rates   b. Rise of the Internet   c. Deregulation   d. Glass-Steagall Act

_____

Outsourcing

Pic 972: Do you think high levels of immigration to the U.S. while simultaneously outsourcing jobs away from the U.S. is sustainable economically? Why or why not?

Graph 972: Which country had the same percentage of women in the workforce in 2016?

Pics 973: Note some of the new 'firsts' for women in the 1990s:

'Pink-collar ghetto'

How did the increasing participation of women in the U.S. workforce economy affect families?

Summarize the Clinton Administration's response to the following foreign crises during the 1990s:

Somalian warlords

Rwandan genocide

Bosnian conflict

Serb-Albanian conflict

Rabin-Arafat talks

Rise of Osama bin Laden and Al Qaeda

Pic 975: What is the USS Cole, and what happened to it?

Whitewater

Lewinsky affair

Pic 976: Read and rate this one, which could be about your grandchildren. Why do you like it?

Pic 976: What was the "Dot-com bubble?"

Map 977: During the 2000 presidential campaign, Al Gore phoned the "most awkward" call in modern history. What was it and why did he make the call?

Who won the popular vote in 2000?

E Pluribus Unum, a traditional American motto, means Of Many, One. Do you think there is a "real American" out there, a way of life, a people, an ideal? Or is the book right to use the term E Pluribus Plures, meaning Of Many, Many to describe us? In your opinion, can we be "united in diversity?" or are we forever to be divided by it?

How were school curriculums changed at the turn of the century to reflect America's growing multiculturalism?

Pic 978: How does this building reflect the postmodernist concept?

Postmodernism

Do you agree with the modernists or postmodernists on "less is more" or "less is a bore"?

Pic 979: In Gone with the Wind, the slave system was depicted humanely, with good feelings shown between the plantation owning family and the slaves who worked it. What is Kara Walker's message in this artwork on the same topic?

Pic 980: Aside from break dancing, think of other aspects of hip-hop culture familiar to you:

REGIME CHANGE
Say my name.

Name _____

YEAR	PLACE	AGAINST	HELPED
1893	Hawaii	Lili'uokalani	Occupation
1898	Cuba	Spain	Occupation
1898	Puerto Rico	Spain	Occupation
1899	Philippines	Aguinaldo	Occupation
1903	Panama	Colombia	Panama
1907	Honduras	Nic. Rebels	Bonilla
1912	Nicaragua	Zelaya	Occupation
1915	Haiti	Cacos	Occupation
1916	Dominican	Jimenes	Occupation
1918	Russia	Lenin	Kornilov
1941	Panama	Arias	Arango
1943	Italy	Mussolini	Gasperi
1944	Greece	NLF	Papandreou
1944	Philippines	Communists	Osmena
1944	Belgium	Grohe	Pierlot
1944	Netherlands	Seyss-Inquart	Beel
1944	France	Petain	de Gaulle
1945	Germany	Hitler	Adenauer
1945	Japan	Meiji	Meiji
1945	China	Mao	Chaing
1949	Syria	Quwatli	Za'im
1950	Korea	PRK	Syngman Rhee
1952	Egypt	Farouk	Nasser
1953	Iran	Mosaddegh	Pahlavi
1954	Guatemala	Arbenz	Armas
1960	Congo	Lumumba	Mobutu
1960	Laos	Le	Nosavan
1961	Dominican	Trujillo	Bosch
1961	Cuba	Castro	Rebels
1961	Brazil	Goulart	Branco
1963	Vietnam	Ngo	Army RSV
1965	Vietnam	Viet Cong	South
1965	Dominican	Cabral	Balaguer
1965	Indonesia	Sukarno	Suharto
1967	Greece	Papandreou	Papadopoulos
1971	Bolivia	Torres	Banzer
1972	Iraq	Saddam	Kurdish rebels
1973	Chile	Allende	Pinochet
1979	Afghanistan	Soviet puppet	Mujahideen
1980	El Salvador	FMLN	
1981	Nicaragua	Sandinista	Contras
1981	Ecuador	Roldos	
1981	Panama	Torrijos	
1983	Grenada	Marxists	
1989	Panama	Noriega	
1991	Iraq	Saddam	Kuwait
1997	Indonesia	Suharto	
2000	Yugoslavia	Milosevic	KLA
2002	Afghanistan	Taliban	Direct
2003	Iraq	Saddam	Direct
2005	Syria	Assad	
2006	Palestine	Haniyeh	
2011	Libya	Gaddafi	Direct
2015	Yemen	Saleh	
2017	Syria	Assad	
2019	Venezuela	Maduro	
2019	Iran	Khamenhi	

Issue _____   **Political Compass**   **Name** _____

You don't get to label me! I'll do it myself.

A	B	C	D	E
State Communism		*Nationalist Socialism*		*Absolutism*
1 Globalism		Fascism		Theocracy 1

2   *Socialism*   2

3 _____ 3

Radical   *Liberal*   *Individual*   *Conservative*   *Reactionary*

4   *Libertarianism*   4

A	B	C	D	E
5				5
Marxist Utopian		*Laissez-Faire Capitalism*		*State of Nature*
A	B	C	D	E

_____ Obey elite commissars who are planning new international society- without countries
_____ Guard the natural rights of life, liberty and property, and make your own free choices within them
_____ This is the original anarchy in which humans found themselves, where only law of the jungle applies
_____ Obey the will of God by supporting the king & clergy members as they manage God's earthly realm
_____ Overturn all traditions and values inherited from the cultural past and wipe the slate clean
_____ Guard stability and traditional values, look to the national and cultural past for guidance
_____ Less government control, less laws and regulations, taxes only for defense, and a self-reliant attitude
_____ Replace old traditions with permissive morality, seek equality of individual and group outcomes
_____ Distrust any change in society, which must be kept the same now as it was in the past
_____ Obey the leaders of your race, as they further your biology through increasing national strength
_____ Abolish government, money, religion, private property and all nations, and live as a pure community
_____ Follow self-interest in a business world free from government regulations, and economy will prosper
_____ More government control, more laws and regulations, higher taxes, but also more services

Place these on the chart: *Washington*   *Mill*   *Robespierre*   *Smith*   *Burke*   *Saud*
     Owen   *Leonidas*   *Lenin*   *Hitler*   *Marx*   *Derrida*   *Caveman*

"I am President Trump, and I approved this message."

Quote 983: If Obama is telling Americans to 'grow up' in this statement, what do you think he means?

_____

WMDs

George W. Bush (43)

Do you agree or disagree with Bush on the following:

That public money should not be used for stem-cell research: _____

That human cloning should be carefully regulated if not banned: _____

That signing the Kyoto Treaty would have been bad for business: _____

That drilling oil in Alaska is better than in the Middle East: _____

That these things should be done regardless of environment: _____

Dick Cheney

Chart 984: Add the combined U.S. budget deficit for each presidential term in the new millennium:

Bush Term 1: 2001 + 2002 + 2003 + 2004:   _____

Bush Term 2: 2005 + 2006 + 2007 + 2008:   _____

Obama Term 1: 2009 + 2010 + 2011 + 2012:   _____

9/11

Pic 985: Note what happened with each of the three hijacked planes:

    Plane 1:   *Plane 2:*   *Plane 3:*

Al Qaeda

Taliban

How was 'asymmetrical warfare' different than conventional warfare?

Patriot Act

Dept. of Homeland Security

Guantanamo

Pg. 987: Examining the Evidence. What about U.S. foreign policy does the National Security Strategy illuminate?

'Axis of Evil'

Neoconservatives

Quote 988: Speaking as a prosecutor, what specific charges is Bush laying on Iraq here?	Did Bush listen to the advice of 'old school' conservatives like Colin Powell and Pat Buchanan, or to neoconservative advisors on the Iraq issue?

Bush went to war without the approval of a majority of Democrats and Republicans in Congress:
 	
    a. True   *b. False*
	It was easier to defeat Iraq militarily and depose Saddam Hussein than to remake Iraq into a modern, democratic nation
	
	    a. True *b. False*

Abu Gharib

Map 989: Iraq, the scene of the oldest settled civilizations in the world, has been inhabited for over 5,000 years. Known as Mesopotamia to historians, most of its major cities lie along its two great rivers. Note the battles fought along both rivers:

    Tigris River: *Euphrates River:*

| Chart 990: Iran is a Shi'a-majority country. Why might someone looking at this chart not be surprised that after the U.S. withdrawal, Iran's influence in Iraq increased dramatically despite the two countries fighting a war in the 1980s? | Quote 990: Do you agree more with the perspective of Bush the elder or Bush the younger on Iraq? Why? |

| Pic 991: This image of a shuffle gaining ground when a bad thing happened in the Middle East means this: | Pg. 992: What city did Hurricane Harvey hit in 2017? |

No Child Left Behind

Deleveraging

Hurricane Katrina

Thinking Globally 990 – Note ways the U.S. has been:

Seen as a hyperpower   *Seen as a hapless power*

| Graph 996: How many months did the Dow take to reach 11,500, the point where it was before the real estate bubble burst and the recession struck? | Note the social consequences of the subprime mortgage bubble bursting: |

American Recovery & Reinvestment Act

ACA

Dodd-Frank

| Map 996: How many 'major' states with 15 electoral votes or over went to the following: | Quote 997: Is Obama optimistic or pessimistic about the times here? |

Obama: *McCain:*

Occupy Wall Street

Pic 999: Describe the atmosphere in the room where, in this historic photograph, the 'top brass' are watching as U.S. Navy Seal Team Six storms the Bin Laden compound in Pakistan:

Chart 1000: Summarize this chart by quintile:

'Occupy Wall Street'

Pic 1002: Obama's campaign slogans were, "Change we can believe in" and "Yes we can." Which amendments does the protester on the left *not* want changed?	| Who do the "99%" in | the other photo want | indicted?	| If you had to be in | either of these pics, | which would it be?

Income gap

Pic 1004: Whose fault is it that this lady is being evicted from the home she mortgaged?

   a. her fault because she didn't pay her mortgage   *b. the bankers for their predatory lending*

   c. the government's fault for not regulating it   *d. maybe a little of all of these*

How many Americans did the iconic company of the mid-20th century, General Motors, employ?

How many does the iconic company of the early-21st century, Apple, employ?

Chart 1000 (top): Which single stat on this chart most surprises you and why?

Chart 1000 (bot.): People who make over 34,823 dollars per year pay this %:

Mitt Romney

Paul Ryan

What was decided in the *Citizens United v. Federal Election Commission* case? | Do you agree with
| the verdict?
|
|

Map 1005: Most counties in the U.S. were   *a. Republican red*   *b. Democrat blue*   in 2012.

The blue voting counties must have   *a. More*   *b. Fewer*   *c. The same*   population as the red.

Pic 1006: Do you predict retirees over 65 will have more or | Graph 1003: When pundits say
less political power in the coming decades? Why? | "we are in uncharted territory"
| regarding government spending,
| what do you think they mean?
_____ |
|
What is an 'unfunded liability?' |
|
_____ |

DACA
_____

In *Arizona v. United States* (2012), the Obama Justice Department under Eric Holder sued the State
of Arizona over a law passed which allowed police to question the legal status of someone they
were searching, and detain them if they were illegal. The Supreme Court took on the case and
ruled in favor of Obama and against Arizona, with the lawyers using the argument that Arizona
was encouraging its officers to use racial profiling. What do you think about this ruling?

_____

What was decided in | Why did same-sex marriage | Why was Obama's NSA
Shelby County v. Holder? | advocates celebrate in 2012? | criticized?
| |
| |
| |
| |
_____ | _____ | _____

Pic 1007: Do you agree with this comic? _____

Freedom Act of 2015 _____

Confirmation bias _____

Iran Nuclear Deal _____

Tax Cuts and Jobs Act _____

Joe Biden _____

Focus on Success Chapter _____   Name _____

Part I: Turn back to the page before the first page of this chapter.
Count the bullet points in the 'Must Understand' section and number that many on this paper; summarize.

Part II: Locate the three prompts in the 'Historical Thinking Skills' section (green box). Write the skill types for this chapter on the lines below, then answer the prompt.

1. _____:

2. _____:

3. _____:

Unit Review Questions for Unit _____   Name _____

1.   2.   3.   4.

5.   6.   7.   8.

9.   10.   11.   12.

13.   14.   15.   16.

17.   18.   19.   20.

Short Answers

1a. _____

_____

_____

1b. _____

_____

_____

1c. _____

_____

_____

2a. _____

_____

_____

2b. _____

_____

_____

2c. _____

_____

_____

Addenda:

Other Materials and

About this Series

DBQ Document Analysis

Investigator_____

What is the prompt of the DBQ?

_____

1. Who wrote D1?	When?	Intended Audience?	POV/Perspective?	Category/Bucket?

Find a clue in D1 that you think will help you answer the prompt:

_____

2. Who wrote D2?	When?	Intended Audience?	POV/Perspective?	Category/Bucket?

Find a clue in D2 that you think will help you answer the prompt:

_____

3. Who wrote D3?	When?	Intended Audience?	POV/Perspective?	Category/Bucket?

Find a clue in D3 that you think will help you answer the prompt:

_____

4. Who wrote D4?	When?	Intended Audience?	POV/Perspective?	Category/Bucket?

Find a clue in D4 that you think will help you answer the prompt:

_____

5. Who wrote D5?	When?		Intended Audience?	POV/Perspective?	Category/Bucket?

Find a clue in D5 that you think will help you answer the prompt:

_____

6. Who wrote D6?	When?		Intended Audience?	POV/Perspective?	Category/Bucket?

Find a clue in D6 that you think will help you answer the prompt:

_____

7. Who wrote D7?	When?		Intended Audience?	POV/Perspective?	Category/Bucket?

Find a clue in D7 that you think will help you answer the prompt:

_____

8. Who wrote D8?	When?		Intended Audience?	POV/Perspective?	Category/Bucket?

Find a clue in D8 that you think will help you answer the prompt:

_____

9. Now that you have examined the documents, look again at the clues they contain and using that data, state a thesis which answers the prompt:

WORD PROJECT BUILDER
Word up

Today we are going to make a project on the Renaissance, Reformation and Scientific Revolution on Microsoft Word.

1. Open Microsoft Word and create a new document.
2. At the top of the page, title your document 'Renaissance Era,' then find and click Insert → Table (3 columns, 6 rows).
3. Across your top row, type 'Humanism' in column 1, 'Vernacular' in column 2, and '95 Theses' in column 3. Center them.
4. Now go online and find a short definition of each of these, and type them into the corresponding boxes in the 2nd row.
5. Next, do an image search for each of the three, locate an *interesting* image, such as a person, art or building that represents humanism as a concept, or a book written in vernacular, and drag it from the Internet into your document's 3rd row.
6. You can resize the images by double clicking on them and making each no more that 2.25 inches wide (the bottom value).
7. Across the 4th row, type 'Council of Trent' in column 1, 'Heliocentric Theory' in column 2, and 'Boyle's Law' in column 3.
8. Now go online and find a short definition of each of these, and type them into the corresponding boxes on the 5th row.
9. Next, repeat Step 5-6 for these new ones, and put their images in the 6th row. All done!
10. Type name / date /hour in the upper right, make sure the document is 1 page only, and print it to media (File → Print).

WORD PROJECT BUILDER
Word up

Today we are going to make a project on the Renaissance, Reformation and Scientific Revolution on Microsoft Word.

1. Open Microsoft Word and create a new document.
2. At the top of the page, title your document 'Renaissance Era,' then find and click Insert → Table (3 columns, 6 rows).
3. Across your top row, type 'Humanism' in column 1, 'Vernacular' in column 2, and '95 Theses' in column 3. Center them.
4. Now go online and find a short definition of each of these, and type them into the corresponding boxes in the 2nd row.
5. Next, do an image search for each of the three, locate an *interesting* image, such as a person, art or building that represents humanism as a concept, or a book written in vernacular, and drag it from the Internet into your document's 3rd row.
6. You can resize the images by double clicking on them and making each no more that 2.25 inches wide (the bottom value).
7. Across the 4th row, type 'Council of Trent' in column 1, 'Heliocentric Theory' in column 2, and 'Boyle's Law' in column 3.
8. Now go online and find a short definition of each of these, and type them into the corresponding boxes on the 5th row.
9. Next, repeat Step 5-6 for these new ones, and put their images in the 6th row. All done!
10. Type name / date /hour in the upper right, make sure the document is 1 page only, and print it to media (File → Print).

WORD PROJECT BUILDER
Word up

Today we are going to make a project on the Renaissance, Reformation and Scientific Revolution on Microsoft Word.

1. Open Microsoft Word and create a new document.
2. At the top of the page, title your document 'Renaissance Era,' then find and click Insert → Table (3 columns, 6 rows).
3. Across your top row, type 'Humanism' in column 1, 'Vernacular' in column 2, and '95 Theses' in column 3. Center them.
4. Now go online and find a short definition of each of these, and type them into the corresponding boxes in the 2nd row.
5. Next, do an image search for each of the three, locate an *interesting* image, such as a person, art or building that represents humanism as a concept, or a book written in vernacular, and drag it from the Internet into your document's 3rd row.
6. You can resize the images by double clicking on them and making each no more that 2.25 inches wide (the bottom value).
7. Across the 4th row, type 'Council of Trent' in column 1, 'Heliocentric Theory' in column 2, and 'Boyle's Law' in column 3.
8. Now go online and find a short definition of each of these, and type them into the corresponding boxes on the 5th row.
9. Next, repeat Step 5-6 for these new ones, and put their images in the 6th row. All done!
10. Type name / date /hour in the upper right, make sure the document is 1 page only, and print it to media (File → Print).

Crash Course* U.S. History Guide

\# _____   *It's Review Time!*   Name _____

Topic of today's episode _____

As the video goes on, summarize a few of the rapid fire points that were *not* covered in the book that seem important:

What topic or theme did "Thought Bubble" portray in this episode?

Why did Mr. Green get shocked (or not) when he read the mystery document?

What was the correct answer?

How did that item tie in to the material in the chapter?

Was there a 'deep' lesson at the very end? What was it?

Test Correction Guide

Time to get it right!

Corrector_____

Test Name_____

Directions: Identify the numbers of the answers you got wrong on the test and write them:

Number	Page in Book	Correct answer (written in the form of a statement using stem of question)

I got most of these wrong because…

History Movie Review

Reviewer _____

What chapter in the book is this movie most appropriate for? _____

The topic(s) it cover(s): _____

Identify some of the key characters in the movie / documentary that embody concepts in the chapter. Describe how the historical issue(s) affect the storyline in the early part of the film.

_____

_____

_____

_____

What was the "low point" or crisis for the main character(s) in the movie? How did the historical issue cause or influence that low point / crisis to occur?

_____

_____

By the end of the movie, it is probable that whatever crises or effects the historical issue was causing was resolved in some way. Explain how this turn of events came about:

_____

_____

_____

Rate this movie from 0-3: _____
3: it was intellectually stimulating and entertaining
2: it had good points but was rather dull
1: it seemed misleading or irrelevant
0: it was not worth seeing- waste of time

Why did you rate it the way you did?

_____

_____

One image or scene that stuck out was:

_____

_____

_____

Would you recommend this movie to friends or relatives outside of history class?

_____

_____

Weekly Planner

Name _____

This week is number: _____

The Main Objective is: _____

Notes and highlights to keep in mind for the test:

_____

_____

_____

_____

_____

_____

_____

_____

_____

_____

_____

_____

_____

_____

_____

_____

_____

Favorite U.S. History Textbooks

In the 19th century when U.S. history began to be taught in schools in a systematic way, George Bancroft had written the standard work, *History of the United States,* on the Colonial Era and the Revolution up to that time. Edward Channing later wrote a standard work, also called *History of the United States,* going through the Civil War. What follows is a list of the top 10 textbooks since, aside from the Bailey/Kennedy/Cohen text we are familiar with.

1. Boyer, Paul et al. *The Enduring Vision.* 1990 and subsequent editions.
   Another very good U.S. history textbook, also still used

2. Brinkley, Alan, *American History.* 1961 and subsequent editions.
   Key text used as a standard work in colleges for many years

3. Boorstin, Daniel. *The Americans (3 vol.).* 1958.
   A Pulitzer-prize winning history of the country

4. Maurois, Andre. *The Miracle of America.* 1944.
   First came Lafayette, then Tocqueville, and then Maurois

5. Muzzey, David Seville. *A History of Our Country.* 1936.
   Taught more students American history than perhaps any other book

6. Van Loon, Hendrik. *America.* 1927.
   Van Loon won the very first Newbery medal, and does all his own art

7. Beard, Charles A. *The Rise of American Civilization (2 vol.).* 1927.
   Bailey called this book "challenging" and it is, classic college text

8. Markham, Edwin. *The Real America in Romance (9 vol.).* 1909.
   Storybook history. Worth it.

9. Fiske, John. *The New World (3 vol.).* 1902.
   One of the big historians, published after his death in History of All Nations by Lea Brothers. Problem with this it is very hard to find. Good luck.

10. Lossing, Benson, *Lossing's New History of the United States (2 vol.).* 1889.
    Classic 19th century American history read in schools and out.

Also, as an addendum to an addendum, we'll add a 'left' and 'right' history.

Left	Right
Zinn, Howard	Paul Johnson
A People's History of the United States	*A History of the American People*
1980	1999

Thank You!

If this resource book has no use for you, it has no value. We strive to make materials you can actually *use*. No waste, no filler, only usable resources with minimal marginalia aligned with the course for convenience. This is how the *Tamm's Textbook Tools* series works:

Coursepak A, the *Assignments* series has daily book-based guided readings for homework or in class. It has the vocab, people and chapter work covered, along with some application and subjective questions.

Coursepak B, The *Bundle* series of bell-ringers, warm ups and openers, available on *Amazon* and elsewhere, has material to be used as grabbers at the beginning of an hour, along with reading comp., online activities if students have computer time, multimedia and video clip response forms, short answers, and tickets-out-the-door. Look for the AP United States History *Bundle* coursepak for Bailey et al. specifically.

Coursepak C, The *Competencies* and *Crossovers* series, is the part of the *Tamm's Textbook Tools* line that goes into more depth on the one hand (competency) and stretches out to connect the disciplines (crossover). If you teach World History, for example, and want a history of the great moments and big ideas in the development of human cultures, or if you want to get an integrated curriculum crossover going with English, Math, Science, Fine Arts, Foreign Languages, or another department of the school, a *Coursepak C: Competencies and Crossovers* might be what you're looking for.

Look for these and more in the *Tamm's Textbook Tools* series, a low-cost, timesaving way to find high quality, custom materials tailor made to textbooks in many different subjects. Contact the marketing department anytime with suggestions, corrections and any other correspondence at hudsonfla@gmail.com. Find *TTT* on Facebook as well. Please inform your colleagues of the existence of this series if you think it will benefit them. Thank you!